NYSTCE 095 ATAS

Assessment of Teaching Assistant Skills
Teacher Certification Exam

By: Sharon Wynne, M.S.
Southern Connecticut State University

XAMonline, INC.
Boston

Copyright © 2008 XAMonline, Inc.
All rights reserved. No part of the material protected by this copyright notice may be reproduced or utilized in any form or by any means, electronic or mechanical, including photocopying, recording or by any information storage and retrievable system, without written permission from the copyright holder.

To obtain permission(s) to use the material from this work for any purpose including workshops or seminars, please submit a written request to:

XAMonline, Inc.
21 Orient Ave.
Melrose, MA 02176
Toll Free 1-800-509-4128
Email: info@xamonline.com
Web www.xamonline.com
Fax: 1-781-662-9268

Library of Congress Cataloging-in-Publication Data

Wynne, Sharon A.
 Assessment of Teaching Assistant Skills 095: Teacher Certification / Sharon A. Wynne. -2nd ed.
 ISBN 978-1-58197-260-3
  1. ATAS Assessment of Teaching Assistant Skills 095.   2. Study Guides.
  3. ATAS   4. Teachers' Certification & Licensure.   5. Careers

Disclaimer:
The opinions expressed in this publication are the sole works of XAMonline and were created independently from the National Education Association, Educational Testing Service, or any State Department of Education, National Evaluation Systems or other testing affiliates.

Between the time of publication and printing, state specific standards as well as testing formats and website information may change that is not included in part or in whole within this product. Sample test questions are developed by XAMonline and reflect similar content as on real tests; however, they are not former tests. XAMonline assembles content that aligns with state standards but makes no claims nor guarantees teacher candidates a passing score. Numerical scores are determined by testing companies such as NES or ETS and then are compared with individual state standards. A passing score varies from state to state.

Printed in the United States of America   œ-1

NYSTCE: ATAS Assessment of Teaching Assistant Skills 095
ISBN: 978-1-58197-260-3

TEACHER CERTIFICATION STUDY GUIDE

Table of Contents

SUBAREA I.   **READING**

COMPETENCY 1.0   UNDERSTANDS THE MEANING OF GENERAL VOCABULARY WORDS 1

Skill 1.1   Determines the meaning of commonly encountered words presented in context 1

Skill 1.2   Identifies appropriate synonyms or antonyms for words 2

Skill 1.3   Recognizes the correct use of commonly misused pairs of words 3

COMPETENCY 2.0   UNDERSTANDS THE STATED MAIN IDEA OF A READING PASSAGE 8

Skill 2.1   Identifies the stated main idea of a passage 8

Skill 2.2   Identifies the topic sentence of a passage 8

Skill 2.3   Recognizes introductory and summary statements of a passage 10

Skill 2.4   Selects an accurate restatement of the main idea of a passage 11

COMPETENCY 3.0   UNDERSTANDS THE SEQUENCE OF IDEAS IN A READING PASSAGE 12

Skill 3.1   Identifies the order of events or steps described in a passage 12

Skill 3.2   Organizes a set of instructions into their proper sequence 12

Skill 3.3   Identifies cause-and-effect relationships described in a passage 13

COMPETENCY 4.0   INTERPRETS TEXTUAL AND GRAPHIC INFORMATION 15

Skill 4.1   Interprets information from tables, line graphs, bar graphs, and pie charts 15

Skill 4.2	Recognizes appropriate representations of written information in graphic or tabular form	16
Skill 4.3	Recognizes differences between fact and opinion	17

SUBAREA II. WRITING

COMPETENCY 5.0 UNDERSTANDS THE STANDARD USE OF VERBS ... 18

Skill 5.1	Identifies standard subject-verb agreement	18
Skill 5.2	Identifies verb tense	19
Skill 5.3	Recognizes consistency of verb tense	20

COMPETENCY 6.0 UNDERSTANDS THE STANDARD USE OF PRONOUNS AND MODIFIERS ... 21

Skill 6.1	Identifies agreement between a pronoun and its antecedent	21
Skill 6.2	Uses possessive pronouns, relative pronouns, and demonstrative pronouns	22
Skill 6.3	Uses comparative and superlative modifiers	25

COMPETENCY 7.0 UNDERSTANDS STANDARD SENTENCE STRUCTURE AND PUNCTUATION ... 26

Skill 7.1	Distinguishes between sentence fragments and complete sentences	26
Skill 7.2	Distinguishes between run-on sentences and correctly divided sentences	27
Skill 7.3	Identifies correct and incorrect punctuation	28

COMPETENCY 8.0 UNDERSTANDS THE STANDARD USE OF CAPITALIZATION AND SPELLING ... 32

Skill 8.1	Identifies standard capitalization at the beginning of sentences	32
Skill 8.2	Identifies standard capitalization of proper words and titles	33
Skill 8.3	Recognizes standard spelling of commonly encountered words presented in context	33

TEACHER CERTIFICATION STUDY GUIDE

SUBAREA III.	MATHEMATICS

COMPETENCY 9.0 UNDERSTANDS NUMBER CONCEPTS 35

Skill 9.1 Identifies the place value of digits 35

Skill 9.2 Identifies correctly rounded numbers 36

Skill 9.3 Identifies equivalent weights and measures in different units 37

Skill 9.4 Estimates the solution to a measurement problem 39

COMPETENCY 10.0 UNDERSTANDS THE ADDITION AND SUBTRACTION OF WHOLE NUMBERS 42

Skill 10.1 Solves problems involving the addition of whole numbers 42

Skill 10.2 Solves problems involving the subtraction of whole numbers 43

Skill 10.3 Applies principles of addition and subtraction of whole numbers to solve problems encountered in everyday life 44

COMPETENCY 11.0 UNDERSTANDS MULTIPLICATION AND DIVISION OF WHOLE NUMBERS 45

Skill 11.1 Solves problems involving the multiplication of whole numbers 45

Skill 11.2 Solves problems involving the division of whole numbers 47

Skill 11.3 Applies principles of multiplication and division of whole numbers to solve problems encountered in everyday life 47

COMPETENCY 12.0 UNDERSTANDS OPERATIONS INVOLVING FRACTIONS, DECIMALS AND PERCENTS 48

Skill 12.1 Solves problems involving fractions 48

Skill 12.2 Solves problems involving decimals 52

Skill 12.3 Solves problems involving percents 56

Skill 12.4 Solves problems involving conversions between fractions, decimals, and percents 57

TEACHER CERTIFICATION STUDY GUIDE

SUBAREA IV.   INSTRUCTIONAL SUPPORT

COMPETENCY 13.0   UNDERSTANDS CLASSROOM INSTRUCTION RELATED TO READING 60

Skill 13.1   Provides support under the guidance of classroom teachers to match student needs, styles of learning, and background experiences 60

Skill 13.2   Helps students use instructional resources to support reading 62

Skill 13.3   Help students use a variety of approaches to understand what they read 65

Skill 13.4   Gathers information about students' progress as readers to support the teacher's planning, assessment, and instruction 70

COMPETENCY 14.0   UNDERSTANDS CLASSROOM INSTRUCTION RELATED TO WRITING 71

Skill 14.1   Understands drafting, editing, and proofreading written work 71

Skill 14.2   Helps students focus their writing 76

Skill 14.3   Helps students use instructional resources to support writing 78

Skill 14.4   Gathers information about students' progress as writers to support the teacher's planning, assessment, and instruction 79

COMPETENCY 15.0   UNDERSTANDS CLASSROOM INSTRUCTION RELATED TO MATHEMATICS 81

Skill 15.1   Relates mathematics to everyday situations 81

Skill 15.2   Identifies and corrects basic errors in addition, subtraction, multiplication, and division 81

Skill 15.3   Helps students use instructional resources to support mathematical learning 84

Skill 15.4   Gathers information about students' progress in mathematics to support the teacher's planning, assessment, and instruction 89

TEACHER CERTIFICATION STUDY GUIDE

Sample Test 91

Answer Key 111

Rigor Table 112

Rationales for Sample Questions 113

I.D.E.A. Update, 2004 153

Study and Testing Tips

In the preface, emphasis was placed upon the idea of focusing on the right material, in other words, *what* to study in order to prepare for the subject assessments. But equally important is *how* you study.

learning n. 1. the acquiring of knowledge of or skill in (a subject, trade, art, etc.) by study; experience, etc. 2. to come to know (of or about) 3. acquired knowledge or skill. *(Definition courtesy of Webster's New World Dictionary of the American Language, 1987)*

What we call learning is actually a very complicated process built around multi-faceted layers of sensory input and reinforcement. When you were a child, learning largely consisted of trial and error experimentation, (i.e., "Don't touch that," "It's *Hot*!" or "This tastes *Good*!").

But as we grow older and the neurotransmitters within our brain develop, learning takes on deeper, subtler levels. As adults the neural pathways are fully in place, allowing us to make abstract connections, synthesizing all of our previous experiences (which is essentially what knowledge is), into tremendously complicated, cohesive thoughts.

However, you can increase your chances of truly mastering the information by taking some simple, but effective steps.

Study Tips:

1. **Some foods aid the learning process.** Foods such as milk, nuts, seeds, rice, and oats help your study efforts by releasing natural memory enhancers called CCKs (*cholecystokinin*) composed of *tryptophan*, *choline*, and *phenylalanine*. All of these chemicals enhance the neurotransmitters associated with memory. Before studying, try a light, protein-rich meal of eggs, turkey, and fish. All of these foods release the memory enhancing chemicals. The better the connections, the more you comprehend.

   Likewise, before you take a test, stick to a light snack of energy boosting and relaxing foods. A glass of milk, a piece of fruit, or some peanuts all release various memory-boosting chemicals and help you to relax and focus on the subject at hand.

2. **Learn to take great notes.** A by-product of our modern culture is that we have grown accustomed to getting our information in short doses (i.e. TV news sound bites or USA Today style newspaper articles.)

Consequently, we've subconsciously trained ourselves to assimilate information better in neat little packages. If your notes are scrawled all over the paper, it fragments the flow of the information. Strive for clarity.

Newspapers use a standard format to achieve clarity. Your notes can be much clearer through use of proper formatting. A very effective format is called the *Cornell Method.* Take a sheet of loose-leaf lined notebook paper and draw a line all the way down the paper about 1-2" from the left-hand edge. Draw another line across the width of the paper about 1-2" up from the bottom. Repeat this process on the reverse side of the page.

Look at the highly effective result. You have ample room for notes, a left hand margin for special emphasis items or inserting supplementary data from the textbook, a large area at the bottom for a brief summary, and a little rectangular space for just about anything you want.

3. **Dissect the material.** Too often we focus on the details and don't gather an understanding of the concept. However, if you simply memorize only dates, places, or names, you may well miss the whole point of the subject.

   A key way to understand things is to put them in your own words. If you are working from a textbook, automatically summarize each paragraph in your mind. If you are outlining text, don't simply copy the author's words. *Rephrase* them in your own words. You remember your own thoughts and words much better than someone else's, and subconsciously tend to associate the important details to the core concepts.

4. **Turn every heading and caption in to a question.** Pull apart written material paragraph by paragraph and don't forget the captions under the illustrations.

   Example: If the heading is "Stream Erosion", flip it around to read "Why do streams erode?" Then answer the questions.

   If you train your mind to think in a series of questions and answers, not only will you learn more, but it also helps to lessen the test anxiety because you are used to answering questions.

TEACHER CERTIFICATION STUDY GUIDE

5. **Read, Read, Read.** Even if you only have 10 minutes, put your notes or a book in your hand. Your mind is similar to a computer; you have to input data in order to have it processed. *By reading, you are storing data for future retrieval.* The more times you read something, the more you reinforce the storage of data.

    Even if you don't fully understand something on the first pass, *your mind stores much of the material for later recall.*

6. **Create the right study atmosphere.** Our bodies respond to an inner clock called biorhythms. Burning the midnight oil works well for some people, but not everyone. If possible, set aside a particular place to study that is free of distractions. Shut off the television, cell phone, pager and exile your friends and family during your study period.

    If you really are bothered by silence, try background music. Not rock, not hip-hop, not country, but classical. Light classical music at a low volume has been shown to aid in concentration. Don't pick anything with lyrics; you end up singing along. Try just about anything by Mozart, generally light and airy, it subconsciously evokes pleasant emotions and helps relax you.

7. **Limit the use of highlighters.** At best, it's difficult to read a page full of yellow, pink, blue, and green streaks. Try staring at a neon sign for a while and you'll soon see my point, the horde of colors obscure the message. A quick note, a brief dash of color, an underline, and an arrow pointing to a particular passage is much clearer than a horde of highlighted words.

8. **Budget your study time.** Although you shouldn't ignore any of the material, ***allocate your available study time in the same ratio that topics may appear on the test.***

TEACHER CERTIFICATION STUDY GUIDE

Testing Tips:

1. **Don't outsmart yourself.** Don't read anything into the question. Don't make an assumption that the test writer is looking for something else than what is asked. Stick to the question as written and don't read extra things into it.

2. **Read the question and all the choices *twice* before answering the question.** You may miss something by not carefully reading, and then re-reading both the question and the answers. If you really don't have a clue as to the right answer, leave it blank on the first time through. Go on to the other questions, as they may provide a clue as to how to answer the skipped questions. If later on, you still can't answer the skipped ones . . . **Guess.** The only penalty for guessing is that you *might* get it wrong. Only one thing is certain; if you don't put anything down, you will get it wrong!

3. **Turn the question into a statement.** Look at the way the questions are worded. The syntax of the question usually provides a clue. Does it seem more familiar as a statement rather than as a question? Does it sound strange? By turning a question into a statement, you may be able to spot if an answer sounds right, and it may also trigger memories of material you have read.

4. **Look for hidden clues.** It's actually very difficult to compose multiple-foil (choice) questions without giving away part of the answer in the options presented. In most multiple-choice questions you can often readily eliminate one or two of the potential answers. This leaves you with only two real possibilities and automatically your odds go to fifty-fifty for very little work.

5. **Trust your instincts.** For every fact that you have read, you subconsciously retain something of that knowledge. On questions that you aren't really certain about, go with your basic instincts, **your first impression on how to answer a question is usually correct.**

6. **Mark your answers directly on the test booklet.** Don't bother trying to fill in the optical scan sheet on the first pass through the test. Just be very careful not to miss-mark your answers when you eventually transcribe them to the scan sheet.

7. **Watch the clock!** You have a set amount of time to answer the questions. Don't get bogged down trying to answer a single question at the expense of 10 questions you can more readily answer

ASSESS. OF TEACH. ASSIST. SKILLS

TEACHER CERTIFICATION STUDY GUIDE

SUBAREA I. READING

COMPETENCY 1.0 UNDERSTANDS THE MEANING OF GENERAL VOCABULARY WORDS

Skill 1.1 Determines the meaning of commonly encountered words presented in context

Context clues help reader determine the meaning of words they are not familiar with. The context of a word is the sentence or sentences that surround the word.

Read the following sentences and attempt to determine the meanings of the words in bold print.

> The **luminosity** of the room was so incredible that there was no need for lights.
>
>> If there was no need for lights then one must assume that the word luminosity has something to do with giving off light. The definition of luminosity is: the emission of light.
>
> Jamie could not understand Joe's feelings. His mood swings made understanding him somewhat of an **enigma.**
>
>> The fact that he could not be understood made him somewhat of a puzzle. The definition of enigma is: a mystery or puzzle.

Familiarity with word roots (the basic elements of words) and with prefixes can also help one determine the meanings of unknown words.

Following is a partial list of roots and prefixes. It might be useful to review these.

Root	Meaning	Example
aqua	water	aqualung
astro	star	astrology
bio	life	biology
carn	meat	carnivorous
circum	around	circumnavigate
geo	earth	geology
herb	plant	herbivorous
mal	bad	malicious
neo	new	neonatal
tele	distant	telescope

Prefix	Meaning	Example
un-	not	unnamed
re-	again	reenter
il-	not	illegible
pre-	before	preset
mis-	incorrectly	misstate
in-	not	informal
anti-	against	antiwar
de-	opposite	derail
post-	after	postwar
ir-	not	irresponsible

Reading in your spare time - newspapers, magazines, novels - can also help to increase your overall vocabulary.

Skill 1.2 Identifies appropriate synonyms or antonyms for words

Synonyms are words that have similar meanings. Sometimes, synonyms can be used in place of another word to make a draft more appealing or descriptive. Teachers should encourage their students to utilize appropriate synonyms when drafting or revising their work to expand the interest and imagery of a written work. Paper or computer thesauruses are helpful in incorporating synonyms into one's writing.

> Examples of synonyms:
> Happy – gay, joyful, ecstatic, content, cheerful
> Angry – irritated, fuming, livid, irate, annoyed
> Beautiful - gorgeous, attractive, striking

However, teachers should also alert students that sometimes one word can not be simply replaced by another just because it was listed as a synonym. Sometimes the meaning or the connotation will vary somewhat. For example, in the sentence "Harold was angry when his brother spilled finger paint on his book report." Replacing "angry" with "fuming" would be a better choice than "annoyed" as the words describe the situation a little differently. As teachers work with students, they can help students expand their vocabularies so students know which synonyms to use.

Antonyms are words that have opposite meanings. As with synonyms, thesauruses will help students identify words that are antonyms.

> Examples of antonyms:
> Sad – cheerful, delighted
> Angry - calm, content
> Beautiful – ugly, repulsive, hideous

Skill 1.3 **Recognizes the correct use of commonly misused pairs of words (e.g., their/there, to/too)**

Students frequently encounter problems with homonyms—words that are spelled and pronounced the same as another but that have different meanings such as *mean*, a verb, "to intend"; *mean* an adjective, "unkind"; and *mean* a noun or adjective, "average." These words are actually both homonyms and homographs (written the same way).

A similar phenomenon that causes trouble is heteronyms (also sometimes called heterophones), words that are spelled the same but have different pronunciations and meanings (in other words, they are homographs that differ in pronunciation or, technically, homographs that are not homophones). For example, the homographs *desert* (abandon) and *desert* (arid region) are heteronyms (pronounced differently); but *mean* (intend) and *mean* (average) are not. They are pronounced the same, or are homonyms.

Another similar occurrence in English is the capitonym, a word that is spelled the same but has different meanings when it is capitalized and may or may not have different pronunciations. Example: *polish* (to make shiny) and *Polish* (from Poland).

Some of the most troubling homonyms are those that are spelled differently but sound the same. Examples: *its* (3d person singular neuter pronoun) and *it's* ("it is"); *there*, *their* (3d person plural pronoun) and *they're* ("they are").

Others: *to, too, two;*

Some homonyms/homographs are particularly complicated and troubling. Fluke, for instance is a fish, a flatworm, the end parts of an anchor, the fins on a whale's tail, and a stroke of luck.

Common misused words:

Accept is a verb meaning to receive or to tolerate. **Except** is usually a preposition meaning excluding. Except is also a verb meaning to exclude.

Advice is a noun meaning recommendation. **Advise** is a verb meaning to recommend.

Affect is usually a verb meaning to influence. **Effect** is usually a noun meaning result. Effect can also be a verb meaning to bring about.

An **allusion** is an indirect reference. An **illusion** is a misconception or false impression.

Add is a verb to mean to put together. **Ad** is a noun that is the abbreviation for the word advertisement.

Ain't is a common nonstandard contraction for the contraction aren't.

Allot is a verb meaning to distribute. **A lot** can be an adverb that means often, or to a great degree. It can also mean a large quantity.

Allowed is used here as an adjective that means permitted. **Aloud** is an adverb that means audibly.

Bare is an adjective that means naked or exposed. It can also indicate a minimum. As a noun, **bear** is a large mammal. As a verb, bear means to carry a heavy burden.

Capitol refers to a city, and capitol to a building where lawmakers meet. **Capital** also refers to wealth or resources.

A **chord** is a noun that refers to a group of musical notes. **Cord** is a noun meaning rope or a long electrical line.

Compliment is a noun meaning a praising or flattering remark. **Complement** is a noun that means something that completes or makes perfect.

Climactic is derived from climax, the point of greatest intensity in a series or progression of events. **Climatic** is derived from climate; it refers to meteorological conditions.

Discreet is an adjective that means tactful or diplomatic, **discrete** is an adjective that means separate or distinct.

Dye is a noun or verb used to indicate artificially coloring something. **Die** is a verb that means to pass away. Die is also a noun that means a cube-shaped game piece.

Effect is a noun that means outcome. **Affect** is a verb that means to act or produce an effect on.

Elicit is a verb meaning to bring out or to evoke. **Illicit** is an adjective meaning unlawful

Emigrate means to leave one country or region to settle in another. **Immigrate** means to enter another country and reside there.

Horde is a verb that means to accumulate or store up. **Horde** is a large group.

ATAS 4

Lead is a verb that means to guide or serve as the head of. It is also a noun that is a type of metal.

Medal is a noun that means an award that is strung round the neck. **Meddle** is a verb that means to involve oneself in a matter without right or invitation. **Metal** is an element such as silver or gold. **Mettle** is a noun meaning toughness or guts.

Morning is a noun indicating the time between midnight and midday. **Mourning** is a verb or noun pertaining to the period of grieving after a death.

Past is a noun meaning a time before now (past, present and future). **Passed** is the past tense of the verb "to pass."

Piece is a noun meaning a portion. **Peace** is a noun meaning the opposite of war.

Peak is a noun meaning the tip or height to reach the highest point. **Peek** is a verb that means to take a brief look. **Pique** is a verb meaning to incite or raise interest.

Principal is a noun meaning the head of a school or an organization or a sum of money. **Principle** is a noun meaning a basic truth or law.

Rite is a noun meaning a special ceremony. **Right** is an adjective meaning correct or direction. **Write** is a verb meaning to compose in writing.

Than is a conjunction used in comparisons; **then** is an adverb denoting time. That pizza is more than I can eat. Tom laughed, and then we recognized him.
Than is used to compare; both words have the letter a in them.
Then tells when; both are spelled the same, except for the first letter.

There is an adverb specifying place; it is also an expletive. Adverb: Sylvia is lying there unconscious. Expletive: There are two plums left. **Their** is a possessive pronoun. **They're** is a contraction of they are. Fred and Jane finally washed their car. They're later than usual today.

To is a preposition; **too** is an adverb; **two** is a number.

Your is a possessive pronoun; **you're** is a contraction of you are.

Strategies to help students conquer these demons: Practice using them in sentences. Context is useful in understanding the difference. Drill is necessary to overcome their misuses.

To effectively teach language, it is necessary to understand that, as human beings acquire language, they realize that words have denotative and connotative meanings. Generally, denotative words point to things and connotative words deal with mental suggestions that the words convey. The word skunk has a denotative meaning if the speaker can point to the actual animal as he speaks the word and intends the word to identify the animal. Skunk has connotative meanings depending upon the tone of delivery, the socially acceptable attitudes about the animal, and the speaker's personal feelings about the animal.

Problem Phrases

Correct	Incorrect
Supposed to	Suppose to
Used to	Use to
Toward	Towards
Anyway	Anyways
Couldn't care less	Could care less
For all intents and purposes	For all intensive purposes
Come to see me	Come and see me
En route	In route
Regardless	Irregardless
Second, Third	Secondly, Thirdly

Other confusing words

Lie is an intransitive verb meaning to recline or rest on a surface. Its principal parts are lie, lay, lain. **Lay** is a transitive verb meaning to put or place. Its principal parts are lay, laid.

> Birds lay eggs.
> I lie down for bed around 10 PM.

Set is a transitive verb meaning to put or to place. Its principal parts are set, set, set. **Sit** is an intransitive verb meaning to be seated. Its principal parts are sit, sat, sat.

> I set my backpack down near the front door.
> They sat in the park until the sun went down.

Among is a preposition to be used with three or more items. **Between** is to be used with two items.

> Between you and me, I cannot tell the difference among those three Johnson sisters.

ATAS

As is a subordinating conjunction used to introduce a subordinating clause; **Like** is a preposition and is followed by a noun or a noun phrase.

> As I walked to the lab, I realized that the recent experiment findings were much like those we found last year.

Can is a verb that means to be able. **May** is a verb that means to have permission. They are only interchangeable in cases of possibility.

> I can light 250 pounds.
> May I go to Alex's house?

COMPETENCY 2.0   UNDERSTANDS THE STATED MAIN IDEA OF A READING PASSAGE

Skill 2.1   Identifies the stated main idea of a passage

A **topic** of a paragraph or story is what the paragraph or story is about.

The **main idea** of a paragraph or story states the important idea(s) that the author wants the reader to know about a topic.

The topic and main idea of a paragraph or story are sometimes directly stated.

There are times, however, that the topic and main idea are not directly stated, but simply implied.

Look at this paragraph.

> Henry Ford was an inventor who developed the first affordable automobile. The cars that were being built before Mr. Ford created his Model-T were very expensive. Only rich people could afford to have cars.

The topic of this paragraph is Henry Ford. The main idea is that Henry Ford built the first affordable automobile.

Skill 2.2   Identifies the topic sentence of a passage

The **topic sentence** indicates what the passage is about. It is the subject of that portion of the narrative. The ability to identify the topic sentence in a passage will enable the student to focus on the concept being discussed and better comprehend the information provided.

You can find the main ideas by looking at the way in which paragraphs are written. A paragraph is a group of sentences about one main idea. Paragraphs usually have two types of sentences: a topic sentence, which contains the main idea, and two or more detail sentences which support, prove, provide more information, explain, or give examples.

You can only tell if you have a detail or topic sentence by comparing the sentences with each other.

Look at this sample paragraph:

Fall is the best of the four seasons. The leaves change colors to create a beautiful display of golds, reds, and oranges. The air turns crisp and windy. The scent of pumpkin muffins and apple pies fill the air. Finally, Halloween marks the start of the holiday season. Fall is my favorite time of year!

Breakdown of sentences:

Fall is the best of the four seasons. (TOPIC SENTENCE)
The leaves change colors to create a beautiful display of golds, reds, and oranges. (DETAIL)
The air turns crisp and windy. (DETAIL)
The scent of pumpkin muffins and apple pies fill the air. (DETAIL)
Finally, Halloween marks the start of the holiday season. (DETAIL)
Fall is my favorite time of year! (CLOSING SENTENCE – Often a restatement of the topic sentence)

The first sentence introduces the main idea and the other sentences support and give the many uses for the product.

Tips for Finding the Topic Sentence

1. The topic sentence is usually first, but could be in any position in the paragraph.

2. A topic is usually more "general" than the other sentences; that is, it talks about many things and looks at the big picture. Sometimes it refers to more that one thing. Plurals and the words "many", "numerous", or "several" often signal a topic sentence.

3. Detail sentences are usually more "specific" than the topic, that is, they usually talk about one single or small part or side of an idea. Also, the words "for example", "i.e.", "that is", "first", "second", "third", etc., and "finally" often signal a detail.

4. Most of the detail sentences support, give examples, prove, talk about, or point toward the topic in some way.

How can you be sure that you have a topic sentence? Try this trick: Switch the sentence you think is the topic sentence into a question. If the other sentences seem to "answer" the question, then you've got it.

For example:
Reword the topic sentence "Fall is the best of the four seasons" in one of the following ways:

"Why is fall the best of the four season?"
"Which season is the best season?"
"Is fall the best season of the year?"

Then, as you read the remaining sentences (the ones you didn't pick), you will find that they answer (support) your question.

If you attempt this with a sentence other than the topic sentence, it won't work

For example:
Suppose you select "Halloween marks the start of the holiday season," and you reword it in the following way:

"Which holiday is the start of the holiday season?"

You will find that the other sentences fail to help you answer (support) your question.

Skill 2.3 Recognizes introductory and summary statements of a passage

The introductory statement should be at the beginning of the passage. An introductory statement will provide a bridge between any previous, relevant text and the content to follow. It will provide information about, and set the tone and parameters for, the text to follow. The old axiom regarding presenting a body of information suggested that you should always "tell them what you are going to tell them; tell it to them; tell them what you just told them." The introductory statement is where the writer will tell the readers what he or she is going to tell them.

The summary statement should be at or near the end of the passage, and is a concise presentation of the essential data from that passage. In terms of the old axiom, the content portion (the main body of the narrative) is where the writer will "tell it to them." The summary statement is where the writer will tell the readers what he or she has just told them.

Skill 2.4 Selects an accurate restatement of the main idea of a passage

An accurate restatement of the main idea from a passage will usually summarize the concept in a concise manner, and it will often present the same idea from a different perspective. A restatement should always demonstrate complete comprehension of the main idea.

To select an accurate restatement, identifying the main idea of the passage is essential (see Skill 2.2). Once you comprehend the main idea of a passage, evaluate your choices to see which statement restates the main idea while eliminating statements which restate a supporting detail. Walk through the steps below the sample paragraph from Skill 2.2 to see how to select the accurate restatement.

Sample Paragraph:
Fall is the best of the four seasons. The leaves change colors to create a beautiful display of golds, reds, and oranges. The air turns crisp and windy. The scent of pumpkin muffins and apple pies fill the air. Finally, Halloween marks the start of the holiday season. Fall is my favorite time of year!

Steps:
1. Identify the main idea. (Answer: "Fall is the best of the four seasons.")
2. Decide which statement below restates the topic sentence:
   A. The changing leaves turn gold, red and orange.
   B. The holidays start with Halloween.
   C. Of the four seasons, Fall is the greatest of them all.
   D. Crisp wind is a fun aspect of Fall.

The answer is C because it rewords the main idea of the first sentence, the topic sentence.

TEACHER CERTIFICATION STUDY GUIDE

COMPETENCY 3.0 UNDERSTANDS THE SEQUENCE OF IDEAS IN A READING PASSAGE

Skill 3.1 Identifies the order of events or steps described in a passage

The ability to organize events or steps provided in a passage (especially when presented in random order) serves a useful purpose, and it encourages the development of logical thinking and the processes of analysis and evaluation.

Working through and discussing with your students examples like the one below help students to gain valuable practice in sequencing events. In the example below, identify the proper order of events or steps:

Example:
1. Matt had tied a knot in his shoelace.
2. Matt put on his green socks because they were clean and complimented the brown slacks he was wearing.
3. Matt took a bath and trimmed his toenails.
4. Matt put on his brown slacks.

The proper order of events is: 3, 4, 2, and 1

Skill 3.2 Organizes a set of instructions into their proper sequence

Students need to be aware of their audience and how their writing comes across to their audience in order to write clearly and in a logical sequence. As with events or steps (discussed in Skill 3.1), the ability to organize a set of instructions into the proper sequence (especially when presented in random order) serves a useful purpose, and it encourages the development of logical thinking and the processes of analysis and evaluation.

Reading the example below proves to be quite confusing to the beginner cook. Proper sequence of events is crucial to ensuring that the meaning of the text is correctly interpreted by the reader. In the example below identify the proper sequence of instructions:

MAKING A YUMMY MACCARONI AND CHEESE DINNER FROM A PACKAGE IS FUN

1. I like mixing in the cheese because that is what makes the dinner so yummy.
2. You must bring the water to a boil in a pot before adding the macaroni.
3. Be sure to add a tablespoon of butter just after you put in the salt.
4. After you strain the cooked noodles, you return them to the pot and add a pinch of salt.
5. After the butter, add the quarter cup of milk.
6. Stir all the ingredients together until the powdered cheese has dissolved into a liquid which evenly coats the macaroni.
7. The macaroni will cook in the boiling water for ten minutes.
8. Of course, the cheese is the last ingredient added—just after the milk.
9. Serve in a big bowl and enjoy!

The proper sequence is: 2, 7, 4, 3, 5, 8, 6, 1, 9.

Skill 3.3 Identifies cause-and-effect relationships described in a passage

Linking cause to effect seems to be ingrained in human thinking. We get chilled and then the next day come down with a cold; therefore, getting chilled caused the cold even though medical experts tell us that the virus that causes colds must be communicated by another human being. Socrates and the other Greek orators did a lot of thinking about this kind of thinking and developed a whole system for analyzing the links between causes and their effects and when they are valid—that is, when such and such a cause did, in fact, bring about a particular effect—and spelled out ways to determine whether or not the reasoning is reliable. When it is not reliable, it is called a fallacy.

A common fallacy in reasoning is the *post hoc ergo propter hoc* ("after this, therefore because of this") or the false-cause fallacy. These errors occur in cause/effect reasoning, which may either go from cause to effect or effect to cause. They happen when an inadequate cause is offered for a particular effect; when the possibility of more than one cause is ignored; and when a connection between a particular cause and a particular effect is not made.

An example of a *post hoc*: Our sales shot up thirty-five percent after we ran that television campaign; therefore the campaign caused the increase in sales. It might have been a cause, of course, but more evidence is needed to prove it.

An example of an inadequate cause for a particular effect: An Iraqi truck driver reported that Saddam Hussein had nuclear weapons; therefore, Saddam Hussein is a threat to world security. More causes were needed to prove the conclusion.

An example of failing to make a connection between a particular cause and an effect assigned to it: Anna fell into a putrid pond on Saturday; on Monday she came down with polio; therefore, the polio was caused by the water in the pond. This, of course, is not acceptable unless the polio virus is found in a sample of water from the pond. A connection must be proven.

TEACHER CERTIFICATION STUDY GUIDE

COMPETENCY 4.0 INTERPRETS TEXTUAL AND GRAPHIC INFORMATION

Skill 4.1 Interprets information from tables, line graphs, bar graphs, and pie charts

Tables

To interpret data in tables, we read across rows and down columns. Each item of interest has different data points listed under different column headings.

Table 1. Sample Purchase Order

Item	Unit	$/Unit	Qty	Total $
Coffee	Lb.	2.79	45	125.55
Milk	Gal.	1.05	72	75.60
Sugar	Lb.	0.23	150	34.50

In Table 1 (above), the first column on the left contains the items in a purchase order. The other columns contain data about each item labeled with column headings. The second column from the left gives the unit of measurement for each item, the third column gives the price per unit, the fourth column gives the quantity of each item ordered, and the fifth column gives the total cost of each item.

Examples: Use Table 1 to answer the following questions.

1. What does the 1.05 value in the table represent?

    Answer: Price in dollars per gallon of milk.

2. What is the total cost of the purchase order?

    Answer: $235.65

3. How many combined pounds of coffee and sugar does this purchase order purchase?

    Answer: 195 lbs.

See also Skill 15.3 for a description of how to create and interpret line graphs, bar graphs and pie charts.

Quantitative data are often easily presented in graphs and charts in many content areas. However, if students are unable to decipher the graph, their use becomes limited to students. Since information can clearly be displayed in a graph or chart form, accurate interpretation of the information is an important skill for students.

For graphs, students should be taught to evaluate all the features of the graph, including main title, what the horizontal axis represents and what the vertical axis represents. Also, students should locate and evaluate the graph's key (if there is one) in the event there is more than one variable on the graph. For example, line graphs are often used to plot data from a scientific experiment. If more than one variable were used, a key or legend would indicate what each line on the graph represented. Then, once students have evaluated the axes and titles, they can begin to assess the results of the experiment.

For charts (such as a pie chart), the process is similar to interpreting bar or line graphs. The key which depicts what each section of the pie chart represents is very important to interpreting the pie chart. Be sure to provide students with lots of assistance and practice with reading and interpreting graphs and charts so their experience with and confidence in reading them develops.

Skill 4.2 Recognizes appropriate representations of written information in graphic or tabular form

Many educational disciplines require the ability to recognize representations of written information in graphic or tabular form. Tables help condense and organize written data and graphs help reveal and emphasize comparisons and trends.

Example: A survey asked five elementary school students to list the number and type of pets they had at home. The first student had three dogs and three fish. The second student had two cats and one dog. The third student had three fish and two dogs. The fourth student had one rabbit, two cats, and one dog. The fifth student had no pets.

Construct a data table and line graph that represent the survey information.

Solution: The following is a table that appropriately represents the data.

Student #	# of Dogs	# of Cats	# of Fish	# of Rabbits	Total # of Pets
1	3	0	3	0	6
2	1	2	0	0	3
3	2	0	3	0	5
4	1	2	0	1	4
5	0	0	0	0	0

TEACHER CERTIFICATION STUDY GUIDE

The following is a line graph that appropriately represents the total number of pets each student has.

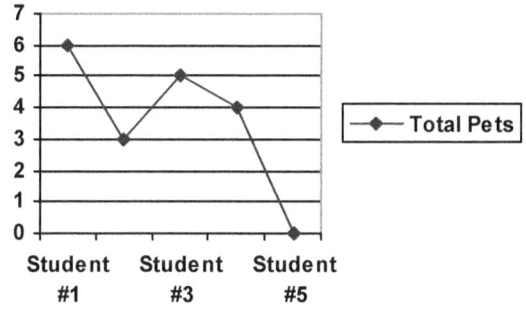

Skill 4.3   Recognizes differences between fact and opinion

A **fact** is something that is true and can be proved.

An **opinion** is something that a person believes, thinks, or feels.

Examine the following examples:

> Joe DiMaggio, a Yankees' center-fielder, was replaced by Mickey Mantle in 1952.
>
>> This is a fact. If necessary, evidence can be produced to support this.
>
> First year players are more ambitious than seasoned players.
>
>> This is an opinion. There is no proof to support that everyone feels this way.

SUBAREA II.   WRITING

COMPETENCY 5.0   UNDERSTANDS THE STANDARD USE OF VERBS

Skill 5.1   Identifies standard subject-verb agreement (e.g., number, person)

A verb must correspond in the singular or plural form with the simple subject; it is not affected by any interfering elements. Note: A simple subject is never found in a prepositional phrase (a phrase beginning with a word such as of, by, over, through, until).

Error: Sally, as well as her sister, plan to go into nursing.

Problem: The subject in the sentence is *Sally* alone, not the word *sister*. Therefore, the verb must be singular.

Correction: *Sally, as well as her sister, plans to go into nursing.*

Error: There has been many car accidents lately on that street.

Problem: The subject accidents in this sentence is plural; the verb must be plural also--even though it comes before the subject.

Correction: *There have been many car accidents lately on that street.*

Error: Everyone of us have a reason to attend the school musical.

Problem: The simple subject is the word *everyone*, not the *us* in the prepositional phrase. Therefore, the verb must be singular also.

Correction: *Everyone of us has a reason to attend the school musical.*

Error: Either the police captain or his officers is going to the convention.

Problem: In either/or and neither/nor constructions, the verb agrees with the subject closer to it.

Correction: *Either the police captain or his officers are going to the convention.*

Skill 5.2   Identifies verb tense (e.g., present, past)

Both regular and irregular verbs must appear in their standard forms for each tense. Note: the ed or d ending is added to regular verbs in the past tense and for past participles.

Error: She should have went to her doctor's appointment at the scheduled time.

Problem: The past participle of the verb *to go* is *gone*. *Went* expresses the simple past tense.

Correction: *She should have gone to her doctor's appointment at the scheduled time.*

Error: My train is suppose to arrive before two o'clock.

Problem: The verb following *train* is a present tense passive construction which requires the present tense verb *to be* and the past participle.

Correction: *My train is supposed to arrive before two o'clock.*

Error: Linda should of known that the car wouldn't start after leaving it out in the cold all night.

Problem: *Should of* is a nonstandard expression. *Of is* not a verb.

Correction: *Linda should have known that the car wouldn't start after leaving it out in the cold all night.*

Skill 5.3 Recognizes consistency of verb tense (e.g., verb endings)

Verb tenses must refer to the same time period consistently, unless a change in time is required.

Error: Despite the increased amount of students in the school this year, overall attendance is higher last year at the sporting events.

Problem: The verb *is* represents an inconsistent shift to the present tense when the action refers to a past occurrence.

Correction: *Despite the increased amount of students in the school this year, overall attendance was higher last year at sporting events.*

Error: My friend Lou, who just competed in the marathon, ran since he was twelve years old.

Problem: Because Lou continues to run, the present perfect tense is needed.

Correction: *My friend Lou, who just competed in the marathon, has run since he was twelve years old.*

Error: The Mayor congratulated Wallace Mangham, who renovates the city hall last year.

Problem: Although the speaker is talking in the present, the action of renovating the city hall was in the past.

Correction: *The Mayor congratulated Wallace Mangham, who renovated the city hall last year.*

COMPETENCY 6.0 UNDERSTANDS THE STANDARD USE OF PRONOUNS AND MODIFIERS

Skill 6.1 Identifies agreement (e.g., number, gender, person) between a pronoun and its antecedent

A **pronoun** is a word that replaces a noun or another pronoun. A pronoun must correspond with the singular or plural form of the noun, called the antecedent, to which it refers. Similarly, a pronoun must be in the same person (1st, 2nd, 3rd) as the noun. A pronoun must refer clearly to a single word, not to a complete idea.

Error: When an actor is rehearsing for a play, it often helps if you can memorize the lines in advance.

Problem: *Actor* is a third-person word; that is, the writer is talking about the subject. The pronoun *you* is in the second person, which means the writer is talking to the subject.

Correction: *When actors are rehearsing for plays, it helps if they can memorize the lines in advance.*

Error: The workers in the factory were upset when his or her paychecks didn't arrive on time.

Problem: *Workers* is a plural form, while *his or her* refers to one person.

Correction: *The workers in the factory were upset when their paychecks didn't arrive on time.*

Error: The charity auction was highly successful, which pleased everyone.

Problem: In this sentence the pronoun *which* refers to the idea of the auction's success. In fact, *which* has no antecedent in the sentence; the word success is not stated.

Correction: *Everyone was pleased at the success of the auction.*

TEACHER CERTIFICATION STUDY GUIDE

Error: Lana told Melanie that she would like aerobics.

Problem: The person that *she* refers to is unclear; it could be either Lana or Melanie.

Correction: *Lana said that Melanie would like aerobics.*

OR

Lana told Melanie that she, Melanie, would like aerobics.

Error: I dislike accounting, even though my brother is one.

Problem: A person's occupation is not the same as a field, and the pronoun *one* is thus incorrect. Note that the word *accountant* is not used in the sentence, so *one* has no antecedent.

Correction: *I dislike accounting, even though my brother is an accountant.*

Skill 6.2 **Uses possessive pronouns (e.g., its vs. it's), relative pronouns (e.g., that, which), and demonstrative pronouns (e.g., this, that)**

Pronouns change case forms. Pronouns must be in the subjective, objective, or possessive case according to their function in the sentence.

Error: Tom and me have reserved seats for next week's baseball game.

Problem: The pronoun *me* is the subject of the verb *have reserved* and should be in the subjective form.

Correction: *Tom and I have reserved seats for next week's baseball game.*

Error: Mr. Green showed all of we students how to make paper hats.

Problem: The pronoun *we* is the object of the preposition *of*. It should be in the objective form, us.

Correction: *Mr. Green showed all of us students how to make paper hats.*

Possessive pronouns

Possessive pronouns indicate possession. Examples of possessive pronouns include *my, yours, his, hers, its, theirs,* and *whose.*

Error: Who's coat is this?

Problem: The interrogative possessive pronoun is whose; *who's* is the contraction for who is.

Correction: *Whose coat is this?*

Relative Pronouns

A relative pronoun relates to a noun preceding it in the sentence. Therefore, it connects a dependent clause to an antecedent (i.e., a noun that precedes the pronoun.) Therefore, the relative pronoun will act as the subject or object of the dependent clause. The relative pronouns are *who, whom, that,* and *which.* You can use relative pronouns to link a phrase or clause to another phrase or clause. Also, when referring to people use these relative pronouns *who* or *whoever* to refer to the subject of the clause, and you can use *whom* or *whomever* to refer to the objects of a verb or preposition.

Error: You may invite *whoever* to the graduation celebration.

Problem: The relative pronoun whoever in this sentence is not replacing the subject of the sentence, but the object to be invited.

Correction: *You may invite whomever to the graduation celebration.*

Error: The voters will choose the candidate whom has the best qualifications for the job.

Problem: The case of the relative pronoun who or whom is determined by the pronoun's function in the clause in which it appears. The word who is in the subjective case, and whom is in the objective. Analyze how the pronoun is being used within the sentence.

Correction: *The voters will choose the candidate who has the best qualifications for the job.*

These pronouns take a different case depending on whether the relative pronoun is a subject or an object in the dependent clause. Therefore, it becomes critical to not only know the subject and object forms of these pronouns but to be able to identify how they are being used in the dependent clause.

Who vs. Whom
When these relative pronouns are the subject (initiating the action) of the dependent clause, use the subjective case (*Who, Whoever*).

When these relative pronouns are the object (receiving the action) of the dependent clause, use the objective case (*Whom, Whomever*).

NOTE: *Who* and *whom* can be interrogative or personal pronouns rather than relative pronouns. In order to be a relative pronoun, it must refer to a noun preceding it.

Which vs. That
When referring to a place, thing or idea, use these relative pronouns (*Which, That*). When using relative pronouns for places, things or ideas, rather than determining case, you must decide whether the information in the dependent clause is essential to the meaning of the dependent clause or simply additional information. When information is critical to the understanding of the main clause, use *that* as the appropriate relative pronoun and do not set the information off by commas. The clause containing the pronoun and not set off by commas is referred to as a restrictive clause.

When information is NOT critical to the understanding of the main clause, use *which* as the appropriate relative pronoun and set the information off by commas. The clause set off by commas is referred to as a nonrestrictive dependent clause. Nonrestrictive relative pronouns describe, add incidental detail or begin new/separate ideas. There is usually a comma separating the non-restrictive clause from the main/independent clause.

Demonstrative Pronouns
A demonstrative pronoun points to and identifies a noun or a pronoun. *This* and *these* refer to things that are nearby either in space or in time, while *that* and *those* refer to things that are farther away in space or time. *This* and *that* are used to refer to <u>singular</u> nouns or <u>noun phrases</u> and *these* and *those* are used to refer to <u>plural</u> nouns and noun phrases.

Skill 6.3 Uses comparative and superlative modifiers (e.g., good/better/best)

A modifier can be an adjective, adverb, phrase or clause that provides more information to another element in the sentence.

Comparative Modifiers
Use the comparative form of an adjective or adverb to compare *exactly* two things. To form the comparative modifier, add the suffix "er" (such as *faster* or *smarter*) to the modifier (for some short words) or by using the word "more" with the modifier. *Better* is also a comparative modifier.

For example:
This pizza is *better* than that pizza.
Michelle was *quicker* to complete the problem than Sarah.
John sells *more* accounts than the rest of the team.

Superlative Modifiers
Use the superlative form to compare three or more things. To form the superlative modifier, add the suffix "est" (such as *tallest* or *biggest*) to the modifier (for some short words) or by using the word "most" with the modifier. *Best* is also a superlative modifier.

For example:
Carla has the *best* working attitude in her department.
In his class, Corey performed with the *most* confidence.
Jennifer has the *biggest* heart of all of my friends.

NOTE: When in doubt as to the appropriate form for the modifier, consult the dictionary. However, there are certain modifiers which you cannot logically use in the comparative and superlative forms. Adjectives like "perfect" and "unique," for instance, express absolute conditions and do not allow for degrees of comparison. Something cannot be *more* perfect than another thing: it is either perfect or not perfect.

TEACHER CERTIFICATION STUDY GUIDE

COMPETENCY 7.0 UNDERSTANDS STANDARD SENTENCE STRUCTURE AND PUNCTUATION

Skill 7.1 Distinguishes between sentence fragments and complete sentences

Fragments occur (1) if word groups standing alone are missing either a subject or a verb, and (2) if word groups containing a subject and verb and standing alone are actually made dependent because of the use of subordinating conjunctions or relative pronouns.

Error: The teacher waiting for the class to complete the assignment.

Problem: This sentence is not complete because an "*ing*" word alone does not function as a verb. When a helping verb is added (for example, was waiting), it will become a sentence.

Correction: *The teacher was waiting for the class to complete the assignment.*

Error: Until the last toy was removed from the floor.

Problem: Words such as until, because, although, when, and if make a clause dependent and thus incapable of standing alone. An independent clause must be added to make the sentence complete.

Correction: *Until the last toy was removed from the floor, the kids could not go outside to play.*

Error: The city will close the public library. Because of a shortage of funds.

Problem: The problem is the same as above. The dependent clause must be joined to the independent clause.

Correction: *The city will close the public library because of a shortage of funds.*

ATAS

Error: Anyone planning to go on the trip should bring the necessary items. Such as a backpack, boots, a canteen, and bug spray.

Problem: The second word group is a phrase and cannot stand alone because there is neither a subject nor a verb. The fragment can be corrected by adding the phrase to the sentence.

Correction: *Anyone planning to go on the trip should bring the necessary items, such as a backpack, boots, a canteen, and bug spray.*

Skill 7.2 Distinguishes between run-on sentences and correctly divided sentences

A run-on sentence consists of two or more independent clauses that have been joined together without a conjunction or the correct punctuation. A run-on sentence will contain two or more independent clauses. Two subjects within the same sentence (or a subject and a pronoun) may indicate a run-on sentence. Run-on sentences can be converted to correctly divided sentences as follows:

- separate the independent clauses/sentences using periods
- add a comma and a conjunction such as and, but, or, so, yet
- place a semicolon between the independent clauses
- change one of the sentences into a clause beginning with because

Review the following run-on sentences, consider how you would correct them and then review the sample corrections.

Examples of run-on sentences
1) He is my best friend he looks after me and takes good care of me.
2) She sleeps all day she studies and writes all night.
3) I'm not sure how she will make out it isn't easy working all night.
4) Of course he likes the idea even so he's unlikely to take on the responsibility unless he's asked to do so.

Corrections
1) He is my best friend. He looks after me and takes good care of me.
2) She sleeps all day because she studies and writes all night.
3) I'm not sure how she will make out; it isn't easy working all night.
4) Of course he likes the idea, but even so, he's unlikely to take on the responsibility unless he's asked to do so.

TEACHER CERTIFICATION STUDY GUIDE

Skill 7.3   Identifies correct and incorrect punctuation

Commas

Commas indicate a brief pause. They are used to set off dependent clauses and long introductory word groups. They are also used to separate words in a series. They are used to set off unimportant material that interrupts the flow of the sentence, and they separate independent clauses joined by conjunctions.

Error: After I finish my master's thesis I plan to work in Chicago.

Problem: A comma is needed after an introductory dependent word-group containing a subject and verb.

Correction: *After I finish my master's thesis, I plan to work in Chicago.*

Error: I washed waxed and vacuumed my car today.

Problem: Words in a series should be separated by commas. Although the word *and* is sometimes considered optional, it is often necessary to clarify the meaning.

Correction: *I washed, waxed, and vacuumed my car today.*

Error: She was a talented dancer but she is mostly remembered for her singing ability.

Problem: A comma is needed before a conjunction that joins two independent clauses (complete sentences).

Correction: *She was a talented dancer, but she is mostly remembered for her singing ability.*

Error: This incident is I think typical of what can happen when the community remains so divided.

Problem: Commas are needed between nonessential words or words that interrupt the main clause.

Correction: *This incident is, I think, typical of what can happen when the community remains so divided.*

ATAS

Semicolons and colons

Semicolons are needed to divide two or more closely related independent sentences. They are also needed to separate items in a series containing commas. Colons are used to introduce lists and to emphasize what follows.

Error: I climbed to the top of the mountain, it took me three hours.

Problem: A comma alone cannot separate two independent clauses. Instead a semicolon is needed to separate two related sentences.

Correction: *I climbed to the top of the mountain; it took me three hours.*

Error: In the movie, asteroids destroyed Dallas, Texas, Kansas City, Missouri, and Boston, Massachusetts.

Problem: Semicolons are needed to separate items in a series that already contains commas.

Correction: *In the movie, asteroids destroyed Dallas, Texas; Kansas City, Missouri; and Boston, Massachusetts.*

Error: Essays will receive the following grades, A for excellent, B for good, C for average, and D for unsatisfactory.

Problem: A colon is needed to emphasize the information or list that follows.

Correction: *Essays will receive the following grades: A for excellent, B for good, C for average, and D for unsatisfactory.*

Error: The school carnival included: amusement rides, clowns, food booths, and a variety of games.

Problem: The material preceding the colon and the list that follows is not a complete sentence. Do not separate a verb (or preposition) from the object.

Correction: *The school carnival included amusement rides, clowns, food booths, and a variety of games.*

Apostrophes

Apostrophes are used to show either contractions or possession.

Error: She shouldnt be permitted to smoke cigarettes in the building.

Problem: An apostrophe is needed in a contraction in place of the missing letter.

Correction: *She shouldn't be permitted to smoke cigarettes in the building.*

Error: My cousins motorcycle was stolen from his driveway.

Problem: An apostrophe is needed to show possession.

Correction: *My cousin's motorcycle was stolen from his driveway.* (Note: The use of the apostrophe before the letter "s" means that there is just one cousin. The plural form would read the following way: My cousins' motorcycle was stolen from their driveway.)

Error: The childrens new kindergarten teacher was also a singer.

Problem: An apostrophe is needed to show possession.

Correction: *The childrens' new kindergarten teacher was also a singer.* (Note: The apostrophe after the "s" indicates that there is more than one child).

Error: Children screams could be heard for miles.

Problem: An apostrophe and the letter s are needed in the sentence to show whose screams it is.

Correction: *Children's screams could be heard for miles.* (Note: Because the word children is already plural, the apostrophe and s must be added afterward to show ownership.)

Quotation marks

Use double quotation marks to enclose a direct quotation and to enclose the title of an article, a song, an essay, or a short story.

Error: Franklin Roosevelt once said, There is nothing to fear but fear itself.

Problem: Double quotation marks are needed to set off the quotation.

Correction: *Franklin Roosevelt once said, "There is nothing to fear but fear itself."*

Error: In his best-selling novel The Firm, published in 1991, author John Grisham probed the sinister doings in a Memphis law firm.

Problem: Double quotation marks are needed to set off the title of an article.

Correction: *In his article, "How to Fish for Trout," Leonard gives good advice to the beginning fisherman.*

Error: In the song Streets of Philadelphia, Bruce Springsteen pays tribute to a man dying from AIDS.

Problem: Use double quotations to set off the title of a song.

Correction: *In the song "Streets of Philadelphia," Bruce Springsteen pays tribute to a man dying from AIDS.*

COMPETENCY 8.0 UNDERSTANDS THE STANDARD USE OF CAPITALIZATION AND SPELLING

Skill 8.1 Identifies standard capitalization at the beginning of sentences

Capital letters are used to indicate specific names of people, places, buildings, companies, courses, products, holidays, days of the week, months, and major sections of the country and the world. Capital letters are also used to signal the start of a sentence and of a direct quotation.

Error: Emma went to Dr. Peters for treatment since her own Doctor was on vacation.

Problem: The use of capital letters with Emma and Dr .Peters is correct since they are specific (proper) names; the title Dr. is also capitalized. However, the word doctor is not a specific name and should not be capitalized.

Correction: *Emma went to Dr. Peters for treatment since her own doctor was on vacation.*

Error: Our Winter Break does not start until next wednesday.

Problem: Days of the week are capitalized, but seasons are not capitalized.

Correction: *Our winter break does not start until next Wednesday.*

Error: The exchange student from israel who came to study biochemistry spoke spanish very well.

Problem: Languages and the names of countries are always capitalized. Courses are also capitalized when they refer to a specific course; they are not capitalized when they refer to courses in general.

Correction: *The exchange student from Israel who came to study Biochemistry spoke Spanish very well.*

Skill 8.2   Identifies standard capitalization of proper words and titles

See Skill 8.1

Skill 8.3   Recognizes standard spelling of commonly encountered words presented in context

Spelling correctly is not always easy because English not only utilizes an often inconsistent spelling system, but also uses many words derived from other languages. Good spelling is important because incorrect spelling damages the physical appearance of writing and may puzzle your reader.

The following is a list of commonly misspelled words:

1. commitment
2. succeed
3. necessary
4. connected
5. opportunity
6. embarrassed
7. occasionally
8. receive
9. their
10. accelerate
11. patience
12. obstinate
13. achievement
14. responsibility
15. prejudice
16. familiar
17. hindrance
18. controversial
19. publicity
20. prescription
21. possession
22. accumulate
23. hospitality
24. judgment
25. conscious
26. height
27. leisurely
28. shield
29. foreign
30. innovative
31. similar
32. proceed
33. contemporary
34. beneficial
35. attachment
36. guarantee
37. tropical
38. misfortune
39. particular
40. yield

I BEFORE E

i before e   grieve, fiend, niece, friend

except after c   receive, conceive, receipt

or when sounded like "a"   as in reindeer and weight, and reign

Exceptions: weird, foreign, seize, leisure

As students acquire and develop spelling skills, they should readily be able to recognize commonly encountered words when presented in context. The practice of recognizing new spelling/study words when presented in context will serve as an aid to improving spelling, pronunciation and understanding of words for most students.

In the sample, below, it is easy to see how the use of spelling/study words in context illustrates any similarities, differences or nuances and may help the student determine the appropriate choice and correct spelling of words.

Sample of Spelling Words within Context
There	Their	They're
Are	Hour	Our
Week	Weak	
Its	It's	
Knight	Night	
Eight	Ate	

We stayed in a very old house in England, during <u>our</u> vacation. It belonged to <u>our</u> friends. <u>They're</u> fortunate to own a manor house. We were <u>there</u> for <u>eight</u> days. <u>There</u> <u>are</u> many interesting things in the house. <u>Their</u> prized possession is a suit of armor which was once worn by a <u>knight</u>. <u>Its</u> helmet had a hinged part that could open or close over the face. We went on a tour of the countryside. <u>It's</u> so beautiful! But we were away for almost <u>eight</u> <u>hours</u>. It was late at <u>night</u> when we got back. I was <u>weak</u> from hunger. I <u>ate</u> enough dinner for two people. Next year, I'm going back to visit for another <u>week</u>.

TEACHER CERTIFICATION STUDY GUIDE

SUBAREA III.   **MATHEMATICS**

COMPETENCY 9.0   UNDERSTANDS NUMBER CONCEPTS

Skill 9.1   Identifies the place value of digits (e.g., hundreds, tens, ones, tenths)

Whole Number Place Value

Consider the number 792. We can assign a place value to each digit.

Reading from left to right, the first digit (7) represents the hundreds' place. The hundreds' place tells us how many sets of one hundred the number contains. Thus, there are 7 sets of one hundred in the number 792.

The second digit (9) represents the tens' place. The tens' place tells us how many sets of ten the number contains. Thus, there are 9 sets of ten in the number 792.

The last digit (2) represents the ones' place. The ones' place tells us how many ones the number contains. Thus, there are 2 sets of one in the number 792.

Therefore, there are 7 sets of 100, plus 9 sets of 10, plus 2 ones in the number 792.

Decimal Place Value

More complex numbers have additional place values to both the left and right of the decimal point. Consider the number 374.8.

Reading from left to right, the first digit (3) is in the hundreds' place and tells us the number contains 3 sets of one hundred.

The second digit (7) is in the tens' place and tells us the number contains 7 sets of ten.

The third digit (4) is in the ones' place and tells us the number contains 4 ones.

Finally, the number after the decimal (8) is in the tenths' place and tells us the number contains 8 tenths.

Skill 9.2 Identifies correctly rounded numbers (e.g., to the nearest ten)

Rounding numbers is a form of estimation that is very useful in many mathematical operations. For example, when estimating the sum of two three-digit numbers, it is helpful to round the two numbers to the nearest hundred prior to addition. We can round numbers to any place value.

Rounding whole numbers

To round whole numbers, you first find the place value you want to round to (the rounding digit) and look at the digit directly to the right. If the digit is less than five, do not change the rounding digit and replace all numbers after the rounding digit with zeroes. If the digit is greater than or equal to five, increase the rounding digit by one and replace all numbers after the rounding digit with zeroes.

Example: Round 517 to the nearest ten.

1 is the rounding digit because it occupies the tens' place.

517 rounded to the nearest ten = 520; because 7 > 5 we add one to the rounding digit.

Example: Round 15,449 to the nearest hundred.

The first 4 is the rounding digit because it occupies the hundreds' place.

15,449 rounded to the nearest hundred = 15,400, because 4 < 5 we do not add to the rounding digit.

Rounding decimals

Rounding decimals is identical to rounding whole numbers except that you simply drop all the digits to the right of the rounding digit.

Example: Round 417.3621 to the nearest tenth.

3 is the rounding digit because it occupies the tenth place.

417.3621 rounded to the nearest tenth = 417.4; because 6 > 5 we add one to the rounding digit.

Skill 9.3 **Identifies equivalent weights and measures in different units (e.g., feet and inches, quarts and pints, kilograms and grams)**

Measurements of length (English system)

12 inches (in)	=	1 foot (ft)
3 feet (ft)	=	1 yard (yd)
1760 yards (yd)	=	1 mile (mi)

Measurements of length (Metric system)

1 kilometer (km)	=	1000 meters (m)
1 hectometer (hm)	=	100 meters (m)
1 decameter (dam)	=	10 meters (m)
1 meter (m)	=	1 meter (m)
1 decimeter (dm)	=	1/10 meter (m)
1 centimeter (cm)	=	1/100 meter (m)
1 millimeter (mm)	=	1/1000 meter (m)

Conversion of length from English to Metric

1 inch	=	2.54 centimeters
1 foot	≈	30 centimeters
1 yard	≈	0.9 meters
1 mile	≈	1.6 kilometers

Measurements of weight (English system)

28 grams (g)	=	1 ounce (oz)
16 ounces (oz)	=	1 pound (lb)
2000 pounds (lb)	=	1 ton (t)

Measurements of weight (Metric system)

1 kilogram (kg)	=	1000 grams (g)
1 gram (g)	=	1 gram (g)
1 milligram (mg)	=	1/1000 gram (g)

Conversion of weight from English to Metric

1 ounce	≈	28 grams
1 pound	≈	0.45 kilograms
	≈	454 grams

ATAS

Measurement of volume (English system)

8 fluid ounces (oz)	=	1 cup (c)
2 cups (c)	=	1 pint (pt)
2 pints (pt)	=	1 quart (qt)
4 quarts (qt)	=	1 gallon (gal)

Measurement of volume (Metric system)

1 kiloliter (kl)	=	1000 liters (l)
1 liter (l)	=	1 liter (l)
1 milliliter (ml)	=	1/1000 liters (ml)

Conversion of volume from English to Metric

1 teaspoon (tsp)	≈	5 milliliters
1 fluid ounce	≈	15 milliliters
1 cup	≈	0.24 liters
1 pint	≈	0.47 liters
1 quart	≈	0.95 liters
1 gallon	≈	3.8 liters

Measurement of time

1 minute	=	60 seconds
1 hour	=	60 minutes
1 day	=	24 hours
1 week	=	7 days
1 year	=	365 days
1 century	=	100 years

Note: (') represents feet and (") represents inches.

TEACHER CERTIFICATION STUDY GUIDE

Skill 9.4   Estimates the solution to a measurement problem (e.g., height, distance, perimeter)

To estimate measurement of familiar objects, it is first necessary to determine the units to use.

Examples:
Length
1. The coastline of Florida
2. The width of a ribbon
3. The thickness of a book
4. The depth of water in a pool

Weight or mass
1. A bag of sugar
2. A school bus
3. A dime

Capacity or volume
1. Paint in a paint can
2. Glass of milk

Money
1. Cost of a house
2. Cost of a cup of coffee
3. Exchange rate

Perimeter
1. The edge of a backyard
2. The edge of a football field

Area
1. The size of a carpet
2. The size of a state

Example: Estimate the measurements of the following objects:

Length of a dollar bill	6 inches
Weight of a baseball	1 pound
Distance from New York to Florida	1100 km
Volume of water to fill a medicine dropper	1 milliliter
Length of a desk	2 meters
Temperature of water in a swimming pool	80° F

ATAS

Depending on the degree of accuracy needed, we can measure an object with different units. For example, a pencil may be 6 inches to the nearest inch or 6 3/8 inches to the nearest eighth of an inch. Similarly, it might be 15 cm to the nearest cm or 154 mm to the nearest mm.

Given a set of objects and their measurements, the use of rounding procedures is helpful when attempting to round to the nearest given unit. When rounding to a given place value, it is necessary to look at the number in the next smaller place. If this number is 5 or more, we increase the number in the place we are rounding and change all numbers to the right to zero. If the number is less than 5, the we leave the number in the place we are rounding the same and change all numbers to the right to zero.

One method of rounding measurements can require an additional step. First, we must convert the measurement to a decimal number. Then, we apply the rules for rounding.

Example: Round the measurements to the given units.

MEASUREMENT	ROUND TO NEAREST	ANSWER
1 foot 7 inches	foot	2 ft
5 pound 6 ounces	pound	5 pounds
5 9/16 inches	inch	6 inches

Convert each measurement to a decimal number, then apply the rules for rounding.

1 foot 7 inches = $1\frac{7}{12}$ ft = 1.58333 ft, round up to 2 ft

5 pounds 6 ounces = $5\frac{6}{16}$ pounds = 5.375 pound, round to 5 pounds

$5\frac{9}{16}$ inches = 5.5625 inches, round up to 6 inches

Estimating Height – The most effective method of estimating height is to compare the height of an object to an object of known height. For example, a student can estimate the height of other students by comparing his height to the height of the other students. To estimate the height of large objects (e.g. trees, buildings), we can take a picture of the object with an object of known height next to it. Then we can use a ruler to estimate the height of the large object by comparison.

Estimating Distance – An effective method of estimating short distances is "stepping off" or "pacing". Walking the distance and counting the number of steps allows us to estimate the distance in yards or meters. An effective method of estimating longer distances is to use objects as points of comparison. For example, we can estimate distance outdoors by noting the apparent size of trees or buildings at our current location and our destination.

Estimating Perimeter – We can estimate the perimeter of geometric shapes by estimating the length of one portion of the shape (e.g. side of a polygon). For example, we can estimate that the perimeter of an octagon with sides measuring approximately one inch is eight inches. We can also estimate the perimeter of large objects, like pieces of property or lakes, by extrapolating from basic measurements. For example, to estimate the perimeter of a lake with a ragged, curved perimeter, we would take straight-line measurements around the edge of the lake and add them together.

COMPETENCY 10.0 UNDERSTANDS THE ADDITION AND SUBTRACTION OF WHOLE NUMBERS

Skill 10.1 Solves problems involving the addition of whole numbers

Addition is one of the four basic number operations. Addition involves the combining of two values or quantities. We call the answer of an addition problem a sum.

The basic algorithm of addition involves aligning numbers by place value and adding each place value column. When a column totals more than ten, we "carry" the tens' digit of the sum to the next column and add it there.

Example: At the end of a day of shopping, a shopper had $24 remaining in his wallet. He spent $45 on various goods. How much money did the shopper have at the beginning of the day?

The total amount of money the shopper started with is the sum of the amount spent and the amount remaining at the end of the day.

```
   24
 + 45
   69
```
→ The original total was $69.

Example: The winner of a race took 1 hr. 58 min. 12 sec. on the first half of the race and 2 hr. 9 min. 57 sec. on the second half of the race. What was the winner's total time?

```
   1 hr. 58 min. 12 sec.
 + 2 hr.  9 min. 57 sec.     Add these numbers
   3 hr. 67 min. 69 sec.
 +        1 min - 60 sec.    Change 60 seconds to 1min.
   3 hr. 68 min.  9 sec.
 + 1 hr.-60 min.       .     Change 60 minutes to 1 hr.
   4 hr.  8 min.  9 sec.  ←  Final answer
```

Example: A biology student counts the number of oranges on three orange trees. The student counted 103 oranges on the first tree, 85 on the second tree, and 122 on the third tree. How many total oranges do the trees contain?

The total number of oranges is the sum of the counts of the three trees.

```
      (1)(1)
       103
        85
     + 122
       310 oranges
```
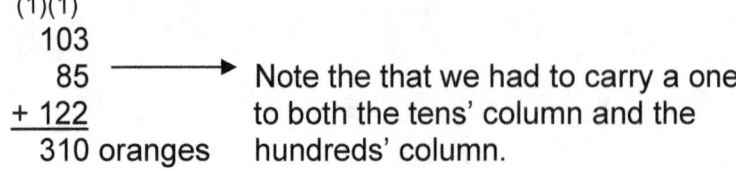
Note the that we had to carry a one to both the tens' column and the hundreds' column.

TEACHER CERTIFICATION STUDY GUIDE

Skill 10.2   Solves problems involving the subtraction of whole numbers

Subtraction is another of the four basic number operations. Subtraction involves taking a quantity or value away from another quantity or value. We call the answer to a subtraction problem the difference.

The basic algorithm for subtraction is the similar to the algorithm for addition. We align the numbers by place value and subtract each column. If the number in the top column is smaller than the number below it, we "borrow" a ten from the tens' column and add it to the top number.

Example: Find the difference of 57 and 39.

$$
\begin{array}{c}
57 \\
-39
\end{array}
\longrightarrow
\begin{array}{c}
57 \\
-39
\end{array}
\longrightarrow
\begin{array}{c}
(5-1=4),\ (7+10=17) \\
4(17) \\
-39 \\
\hline
18
\end{array}
$$

Note that because 7 is less than 9 we borrow a ten from the 5 in the tens' column. This leaves a 4 and adding ten to the 7 produces 17. Thus, $17 - 9 = 8$ and $4 - 3 = 1$. The final difference is 18.

Example: At the end of his shift, a cashier has $96 in the cash register. At the beginning of his shift, he had $15. How much money did the cashier collect during his shift?

The total collected is the difference of the ending amount and the starting amount.

$$
\begin{array}{r}
96 \\
-\ 15 \\
\hline
81
\end{array}
$$

The total collected was $81.

Skill 10.3   Applies principles of addition and subtraction of whole numbers to solve problems encountered in everyday life

See Skills 10.1 and 10.2.

TEACHER CERTIFICATION STUDY GUIDE

COMPETENCY 11.0 UNDERSTANDS MULTIPLICATION AND DIVISION OF WHOLE NUMBERS

Skill 11.1 Solves problems involving the multiplication of whole numbers

Multiplication is one of the four basic number operations. In simple terms, multiplication is the addition of a number to itself a certain number of times. For example, 4 multiplied by 3 is the equal to 4 + 4 + 4 or 3 + 3 + 3 +3. Another way of conceptualizing multiplication is to think in terms of groups. For example, if we have 4 groups of 3 students, the total number of students is 4 multiplied by 3. We call the solution to a multiplication problem the product.

The basic algorithm for whole number multiplication begins with aligning the numbers by place value with the number containing more places on top.

$$\begin{array}{r} 172 \\ \times\ 43 \end{array}$$ ⟶ Note that we placed 122 on top because it has more places than 43 does.

Next, we multiply the ones' place of the second number by each place value of the top number sequentially.

$$\begin{array}{r} (2) \\ 172 \\ \times\ 43 \\ \hline 516 \end{array}$$ ⟶ {3 x 2 = 6, 3 x 7 = 21, 3 x 1 = 3}
Note that we had to carry a 2 to the hundreds' column because 3 x 7 = 21. Note also that we add, not multiply, carried numbers to the product.

Next, we multiply the number in the tens' place of the second number by each place value of the top number sequentially. Because we are multiplying by a number in the tens' place, we place a zero at the end of this product.

$$\begin{array}{r} (2) \\ 172 \\ \times\ 43 \\ \hline 516 \\ 6880 \end{array}$$ ⟶ {4 x 2 = 8, 4 x 7 = 28, 4 x 1 = 4}

Finally, to determine the final product we add the two partial products.

$$\begin{array}{r} 172 \\ \times\ 43 \\ \hline 516 \\ +\ 6880 \\ \hline 7396 \end{array}$$ ⟶ The product of 172 and 43 is 7396.

ATAS

Example: A student buys 4 boxes of crayons. Each box contains 16 crayons. How many total crayons does the student have?

The total number of crayons is 16 x 4.

$$\begin{array}{r} 16 \\ \times\ 4 \\ \hline 64 \end{array}$$ → Total number of crayons equals 64.

Skill 11.2 Solves problems involving the division of whole numbers

Division, the inverse of multiplication, is another of the four basic number operations. When we divide one number by another, we determine how many times we can multiply the divisor (number divided by) before we exceed the number we are dividing (dividend). For example, 8 divided by 2 equals 4 because we can multiply 2 four times to reach 8 (2 x 4 = 8 or 2 + 2 + 2 + 2 = 8). Using the grouping conceptualization we used with multiplication, we can divide 8 into 4 groups of 2 or 2 groups of 4. We call the answer to a division problem the quotient.

If the divisor does not divide evenly into the dividend, we express the leftover amount either as a remainder or as a fraction with the divisor as the denominator. For example, 9 divided by 2 equals 4 with a remainder of 1 or 4 ½.

The basic algorithm for division is long division. We start by representing the quotient as follows.

$14\overline{)293}$ → 14 is the divisor and 293 is the dividend.
This represents 293 ÷ 14.

Next, we divide the divisor into the dividend starting from the left.

$14\overline{)293}$ with 2 above → 14 divides into 29 two times with a remainder.

Next, we multiply the partial quotient by the divisor, subtract this value from the first digits of the dividend, and bring down the remaining dividend digits to complete the number.

$$\begin{array}{r} 2 \\ 14\overline{)293} \\ -28 \\ \hline 13 \end{array}$$ → 2 x 14 = 28, 29 – 28 = 1, and bringing down the 3 yields 13.

Finally, we divide again (the divisor into the remaining value) and repeat the preceding process. The number left after the subtraction represents the remainder.

$$\begin{array}{r} 20 \\ 14\overline{)293} \\ -28 \\ \hline 13 \\ -0 \\ \hline 13 \end{array}$$

→ The final quotient is 20 with a remainder of 13. We can also represent this quotient as 20 13/14.

Example: Each box of apples contains 24 apples. How many boxes must a grocer purchase to supply a group of 252 people with one apple each?

The grocer needs 252 apples. Because he must buy apples in groups of 24, we divide 252 by 24 to determine how many boxes he needs to buy.

$$\begin{array}{r} 10 \\ 24\overline{)252} \\ -24 \\ \hline 12 \\ -0 \\ \hline 12 \end{array}$$

→ The quotient is 10 with a remainder of 12.

Thus, the grocer needs 10 boxes plus 12 more apples. Therefore, the minimum number of boxes the grocer can purchase is 11.

Example: At his job, John gets paid $20 for every hour he works. If John made $940 in a week, how many hours did he work?

This is a division problem. To determine the number of hours John worked, we divide the total amount made ($940) by the hourly rate of pay ($20). Thus, the number of hours worked equals 940 divided by 20.

$$\begin{array}{r} 47 \\ 20\overline{)940} \\ \underline{-80} \\ 140 \\ \underline{-140} \\ 0 \end{array}$$

→ 20 divides into 940, 47 times with no remainder.

John worked 47 hours.

Skill 11.3 **Applies principles of multiplication and division of whole numbers to solve problems encountered in everyday life**

See Skills 11.1 and 11.2.

TEACHER CERTIFICATION STUDY GUIDE

COMPETENCY 12.0 UNDERSTANDS OPERATIONS INVOLVING

Skill 12.1 Solves problems involving fractions (e.g., recipes)

A fraction is a part of a whole number. The denominator (bottom number of a fraction) tells us how many parts we are dividing the whole into and the numerator (top number of a fraction) tells us how many whole parts we are dealing with.

Addition and subtraction of fractions

Key Points

1. You need a common denominator in order to add and subtract reduced and improper fractions.

   Example: $\dfrac{1}{3} + \dfrac{7}{3} = \dfrac{1+7}{3} = \dfrac{8}{3} = 2\dfrac{2}{3}$

   Example: $\dfrac{4}{12} + \dfrac{6}{12} - \dfrac{3}{12} = \dfrac{4+6-3}{12} = \dfrac{7}{12}$

2. Adding an integer and a fraction of the <u>same</u> sign results directly in a mixed fraction.

   Example: $2 + \dfrac{2}{3} = 2\dfrac{2}{3}$

   Example: $^-2 - \dfrac{3}{4} = ^- 2\dfrac{3}{4}$

3. Adding an integer and a fraction with different signs involves the following steps.

   -get a common denominator
   -add or subtract as needed
   -change to a mixed fraction if possible

   Example: $2 - \dfrac{1}{3} = \dfrac{2 \times 3 - 1}{3} = \dfrac{6-1}{3} = \dfrac{5}{3} = 1\dfrac{2}{3}$

ATAS

Example: Add $7\frac{3}{8} + 5\frac{2}{7}$

Add the whole numbers; add the fractions and combine the two results:

$$7\frac{3}{8} + 5\frac{2}{7} = (7+5) + (\frac{3}{8} + \frac{2}{7})$$
$$= 12 + \frac{(7 \times 3) + (8 \times 2)}{56} \quad \text{(LCM of 8 and 7)}$$
$$= 12 + \frac{21 + 16}{56} = 12 + \frac{37}{56} = 12\frac{37}{56}$$

Example: Perform the operation.

$$\frac{2}{3} - \frac{5}{6}$$

We first find the LCM of 3 and 6 which is 6.

$$\frac{2 \times 2}{3 \times 2} - \frac{5}{6} \rightarrow \frac{4-5}{6} = \frac{^-1}{6} \quad \text{(Using method A)}$$

Example: $^-7\frac{1}{4} + 2\frac{7}{8}$

$$^-7\frac{1}{4} + 2\frac{7}{8} = (^-7 + 2) + (\frac{^-1}{4} + \frac{7}{8})$$

$$= (^-5) + \frac{(^-2 + 7)}{8} = (^-5) + (\frac{5}{8})$$

$$= (^-5) + \frac{5}{8} = \frac{^-5 \times 8}{1 \times 8} + \frac{5}{8} = \frac{^-40 + 5}{8}$$

$$= \frac{^-35}{8} = ^-4\frac{3}{8}$$

Divide 35 by 8 to get 4, remainder 3.

Caution: Common error would be

$$-7\frac{1}{4} + 2\frac{7}{8} = -7\frac{2}{8} + 2\frac{7}{8} = -5\frac{9}{8} \quad \text{Wrong.}$$

It is correct to add -7 and 2 to get -5, but adding $\frac{2}{8} + \frac{7}{8} = \frac{9}{8}$ is wrong. It should have been $\frac{-2}{8} + \frac{7}{8} = \frac{5}{8}$. Then,

$$-5 + \frac{5}{8} = -4\frac{3}{8} \quad \text{as before.}$$

Multiplication of fractions

Using the following example: $3\frac{1}{4} \times \frac{5}{6}$

1. Convert each number to an improper fraction.

$$3\frac{1}{4} = \frac{(12+1)}{4} = \frac{13}{4} \qquad \frac{5}{6} \text{ is already in reduced form.}$$

2. Reduce (cancel) common factors of the numerator and denominator if they exist.

$$\frac{13}{4} \times \frac{5}{6} \quad \text{No common factors exist.}$$

3. Multiply the numerators by each other and the denominators by each other.

$$\frac{13}{4} \times \frac{5}{6} = \frac{65}{24}$$

4. If possible, reduce the fraction back to its lowest term.

$$\frac{65}{24} \quad \text{Cannot be reduced further.}$$

5. Convert the improper fraction back to a mixed fraction by using long division.

$$\frac{65}{24} = 24\overline{)65} \qquad = 2\frac{17}{24}$$
$$\phantom{\frac{65}{24} = 24)}\underline{48}$$
$$\phantom{\frac{65}{24} = 24)6}17$$

ATAS

Summary of sign changes for multiplication:

a. $(+) \times (+) = (+)$

b. $(-) \times (+) = (-)$

c. $(+) \times (-) = (-)$

d. $(-) \times (-) = (+)$

Example: $7\dfrac{1}{3} \times \dfrac{5}{11} = \dfrac{22}{3} \times \dfrac{5}{11}$ Reduce like terms (22 and 11)

$$= \dfrac{2}{3} \times \dfrac{5}{1} = \dfrac{10}{3} = 3\dfrac{1}{3}$$

Example: $-6\dfrac{1}{4} \times \dfrac{5}{9} = \dfrac{-25}{4} \times \dfrac{5}{9}$

$$= \dfrac{-125}{36} = -3\dfrac{17}{36}$$

Example: $\dfrac{-1}{4} \times \dfrac{-3}{7}$ Negative times a negative equals positive.

$$= \dfrac{1}{4} \times \dfrac{3}{7} = \dfrac{3}{28}$$

Division of fractions:

1. Change mixed fractions to improper fraction.

2. Change the division problem to a multiplication problem by using the reciprocal of the number after the division sign.

3. Find the sign of the final product.

4. Cancel if common factors exist between the numerator and the denominator.

5. Multiply the numerators together and the denominators together.

6. Change the improper fraction to a mixed number.

Example: $3\dfrac{1}{5} \div 2\dfrac{1}{4} = \dfrac{16}{5} \div \dfrac{9}{4}$

$= \dfrac{16}{5} \times \dfrac{4}{9}$ Reciprocal of $\dfrac{9}{4}$ is $\dfrac{4}{9}$.

$= \dfrac{64}{45} = 1\dfrac{19}{45}$

Example: $7\dfrac{3}{4} \div 11\dfrac{5}{8} = \dfrac{31}{4} \div \dfrac{93}{8}$

$= \dfrac{31}{4} \times \dfrac{8}{93}$ Reduce like terms.

$= \dfrac{1}{1} \times \dfrac{2}{3} = \dfrac{2}{3}$

Example: $\left(^-2\dfrac{1}{2}\right) \div 4\dfrac{1}{6} = \dfrac{^-5}{2} \div \dfrac{25}{6}$

$= \dfrac{^-5}{2} \times \dfrac{6}{25}$ Reduce like terms.

$= \dfrac{^-1}{1} \times \dfrac{3}{5} = \dfrac{^-3}{5}$

Example: $\left(^-5\dfrac{3}{8}\right) \div \left(\dfrac{^-7}{16}\right) = \dfrac{^-43}{8} \div \dfrac{^-7}{16}$

$= \dfrac{^-43}{8} \times \dfrac{^-16}{7}$ Reduce like terms.

$= \dfrac{43}{1} \times \dfrac{2}{7}$ Negative times a negative equals a positive.

$= \dfrac{86}{7} = 12\dfrac{2}{7}$

Skill 12.2   Solves problems involving decimals (e.g., money)

When we complete the division of fractions, we produce decimal numbers. For example, we can express the fraction ½ as 0.5. Operations with decimals are similar to whole numbers with a few key differences.

Addition and Subtraction of Decimals

When adding and subtracting decimals, we align the numbers by place value as we do with whole numbers. After adding or subtracting each column, we bring the decimal down, placing it in the same location as in the numbers added or subtracted.

Example: Find the sum of 152.3 and 36.342.

$$\begin{array}{r} 152.300 \\ +36.342 \\ \hline 188.642 \end{array}$$

Note that we placed two zeroes after the final place value in 152.3 to clarify the column addition.

Example: Find the difference of 152.3 and 36.342.

$$\begin{array}{r} 2910 \\ 152.300 \\ -36.342 \\ \hline 58 \end{array} \longrightarrow \begin{array}{r} (4)11(12) \\ 152.300 \\ -36.342 \\ \hline 115.958 \end{array}$$

Note how we borrowed to subtract from the zeroes in the hundredths' and thousandths' place of 152.300.

TEACHER CERTIFICATION STUDY GUIDE

Multiplication of Decimals

When multiplying decimal numbers, we multiply exactly as with whole numbers and place the decimal moving in from the left the total number of decimal places contained in the two numbers multiplied. For example, when multiplying 1.5 and 2.35, we place the decimal in the product 3 places in from the left (3.525).

Example: Find the product of 3.52 and 4.1.

```
        3.52  ──►  Note that there are 3 total decimal places
      x 4.1         in the two numbers.
        352
    + 14080
      14432  ──►  We place the decimal 3 places in from the
                   left.
```

Thus, the final product is 14.432.

Example: A shopper has 5 one-dollar bills, 6 quarters, 3 nickels, and 4 pennies in his pocket. How much money does he have?

```
                          3
  5 x $1.00 = $5.00    $0.25    $0.05    $0.01
                       x   6    x   3    x   4
                       $1.50    $0.15    $0.04
```

Note the placement of the decimals in the multiplication products. Thus, the total amount of money in the shopper's pocket is:

```
    $5.00
     1.50
     0.15
  +  0.04
    $6.69
```

Division of Decimals

When dividing decimal numbers, we first remove the decimal in the divisor by moving the decimal in the dividend the same number of spaces to the right. For example, when dividing 1.45 into 5.3 we convert the numbers to 145 and 530 and perform normal whole number division.

Example: Find the quotient of 5.3 divided by 1.45.
Convert to 145 and 530.

Divide.

$$145\overline{)530} \quad \begin{array}{r} 3 \\ -435 \\ \hline 95 \end{array} \longrightarrow 145\overline{)530.00} \quad \begin{array}{r} 3.65 \\ -435 \\ \hline 950 \\ -870 \\ \hline 800 \end{array}$$

Note that we insert the decimal to continue division.

Because one of the numbers divided contained one decimal place, we round the quotient to one decimal place. Thus, the final quotient is 3.7.

Applied Problem Solving

The most common use of decimals in everyday life is money. Consider the following problem dealing with a money transaction.

Question: A shopper has 5 one-dollar bills, 6 quarters, 3 nickels, and 4 pennies in his pocket. How much money does he have?

Solution:

$$5 \times \$1.00 = \$5.00 \qquad \begin{array}{r} 3 \\ \$0.25 \\ \times 6 \\ \hline \$1.50 \end{array} \qquad \begin{array}{r} \$0.05 \\ \times 3 \\ \hline \$0.15 \end{array} \qquad \begin{array}{r} \$0.01 \\ \times 4 \\ \hline \$0.04 \end{array}$$

Note the placement of the decimals in the multiplication products. Thus, the total amount of money in the shopper's pocket is:

$$\begin{array}{r} \$5.00 \\ 1.50 \\ 0.15 \\ + 0.04 \\ \hline \$6.69 \end{array}$$

TEACHER CERTIFICATION STUDY GUIDE

Skill 12.3   Solves problems involving percents (e.g., grades, discounts)

Percent means per 100 (%).

Example: 10 percent $= \dfrac{10}{100} = \dfrac{1}{10} = 0.1$

Example: 10 percent of 150 means $\dfrac{10}{100} \times \dfrac{150}{1} = 15$

Example: Add 75% of 25 to 10% of 1000.

$$75\% \text{ of } 25 = \dfrac{75}{100} \times \dfrac{25}{1} = \dfrac{75}{4} \times \dfrac{1}{1} = \dfrac{75}{4} = 18\dfrac{3}{4} \text{ and}$$

$$10\% \text{ of } 1000 = \dfrac{10}{100} \times \dfrac{1000}{1} = \dfrac{10}{1} \times \dfrac{10}{1} = 100$$

Adding the two numbers gives:

$$18\dfrac{3}{4} + 100 = 118\dfrac{3}{4} \text{ or } 118.75$$

Example: 5 is what percent of 20?

This is the same as converting $\dfrac{5}{20}$ to % form.

$$\dfrac{5}{20} \times \dfrac{100}{1} = \dfrac{5}{1} \times \dfrac{5}{1} = 25\%$$

Example: There are 64 dogs in the kennel. 48 are collies. What percent are collies?

Restate the problem.   48 is what percent of 64?
Write an equation. $48 = n \times 64$
Solve. $\dfrac{48}{64} = n$

$n = \dfrac{3}{4} = 75\%$

75% of the dogs are collies.

ATAS

Example: The auditorium was filled to 90% capacity. There were 558 seats occupied. What is the capacity of the auditorium?

Restate the problem. 90% of what number is 558?
Write an equation. $0.9n = 558$
Solve. $n = \frac{558}{.9}$
                      $n = 620$

The capacity of the auditorium is 620 people.

Example: A pair of shoes costs $42.00. Sales tax is 6%. What is the total cost of the shoes?

Restate the problem. What is 6% of 42?
Write an equation. $n = 0.06 \times 42$
Solve. $n = 2.52$

Add the sales tax to the cost. $42.00 + $2.52 = $44.52

The total cost of the shoes, including sales tax, is $44.52.

Skill 12.4 Solves problems involving conversions between fractions, decimals, and percents

A **decimal** can be converted to a **percent** by multiplying by 100, or merely moving the decimal point two places to the right. A **percent** can be converted to a **decimal** by dividing by 100, or moving the decimal point two places to the left.

Examples: 0.375 = 37.5%
0.7 = 70%
0.04 = 4 %
3.15 = 315 %
84% = 0.84
3 % = 0.03
60% = 0.6
110% = 1.1
$\frac{1}{2}$% = 0.5% = 0.005

TEACHER CERTIFICATION STUDY GUIDE

A **percent** can be converted to a **fraction** by placing it over 100 and reducing to simplest terms.

Example: Convert 0.056 to a fraction.

Multiplying 0.056 by $\dfrac{1000}{1000}$ to get rid of the decimal point:

$$0.056 \times \frac{1000}{1000} = \frac{56}{1000} = \frac{7}{125}$$

Example: Find 23% of 1000.

$$= \frac{23}{100} \times \frac{1000}{1} = 23 \times 10 = 230$$

Example: Convert 6.25% to a decimal and to a fraction.

$$6.25\% = 0.0625 = 0.0625 \times \frac{10000}{10000} = \frac{625}{10000} = \frac{1}{16}$$

Example: Find the decimal equivalent of $\dfrac{7}{10}$.

$$\begin{array}{r} .7 \\ 10\overline{)7.0} \\ \underline{70} \\ 00 \end{array}$$

Since 10 cannot divide into 7 evenly, put a decimal point in the answer row on top; put a zero behind 7 to make it 70. Continue the division process. If a remainder occurs, put a zero by the last digit of the remainder and continue the division.

Thus $\dfrac{7}{10} = 0.7$

It is a good idea to write a zero before the decimal point so that the decimal point is emphasized.

Example: Find the decimal equivalent of $\frac{7}{125}$.

$$\begin{array}{r} .056 \\ 125\overline{)7.000} \\ \underline{625} \\ 750 \\ \underline{750} \\ 0 \end{array}$$

An example of a type of problem involving fractions is the conversion of recipes. For example, if a recipe serves 8 people and we want to make enough to serve only 4, we must determine how much of each ingredient to use. The conversion factor, the number we multiply each ingredient by, is:

$$\text{Conversion Factor} = \frac{\text{Number of Servings Needed}}{\text{Number of Servings in Recipe}}$$

Example: Consider the following recipe.

3 cups flour
½ tsp. baking powder
2/3 cups butter
2 cups sugar
2 eggs

If the above recipe serves 8, how much of each ingredient do we need to serve only 4 people?

First, determine the conversion factor.

$$\text{Conversion Factor} = \frac{4}{8} = \frac{1}{2}$$

Next, multiply each ingredient by the conversion factor.

3 x ½ =   1 ½ cups flour
½ x ½ =   ¼ tsp. baking powder
2/3 x ½ = 2/6 =   1/3 cups butter
2 x ½ =   1 cup sugar
2 x ½ =   1 egg

TEACHER CERTIFICATION STUDY GUIDE

SUBAREA IV.   **INSTRUCTIONAL SUPPORT**

COMPETENCY 13.0   **UNDERSTANDS CLASSROOM INSTRUCTION RELATED TO READING**

Skill 13.1   **Provides support under the guidance of classroom teachers to match student needs, styles of learning, and background experiences (e.g., drilling, using pictorial or video materials, relating reading materials to real-life contexts)**

The classroom teacher (in conjunction with other faculty and support staff, as necessary, will identify and define the specific needs of individual students regarding each student's acquisition of reading skills appropriate to the grade level. Using this direction provided by the teacher, the teaching assistant can work effectively with individual students or groups, as assigned, to ensure these needs are met. High expectations for student achievement, which are age-appropriate and focused, provide the foundation for a positive relationship with young students and are consistent with effective instructional strategies.

It is equally important to determine what is appropriate for specific individuals in the classroom and approach classroom groups and individual students with an understanding and respect for their emerging capabilities. Those who study childhood development recognize that young students grow and mature in common, recognizable patterns, but at different rates which cannot be effectively accelerated. This can result in variance in the reading performance of different children in the same classroom. With the establishment of inclusion as a standard in the classroom, it is necessary to understand that variation in development among the student population is another aspect of diversity within the classroom. This has implications for the ways in which instruction is planned and delivered and the ways in which students learn and are evaluated.

Young children are continually developing physically, emotionally and intellectually. Even among peers in a classroom setting there can be diverse levels of development. Furthermore, not all young minds are cognitively receptive to the same degree at the same age or grade level. Providing all students with the same knowledge base and the same reading skills can be challenging in a cognitively diverse classroom. The classroom teacher must plan according to the norm, allowing for exceptions which ensure the inclusion of all students in the education process. Teaching assistants can provide the support which will enable the teacher to meet this objective.

ATAS

The requirement for students within a diverse classroom to acquire the same academic skills (at the same levels) can sometimes be achieved with programmed learning materials. The nature of these materials allows for more individual attention than traditional classroom instruction, as each student starts from his or her evaluated level of need and works through the program to attain the skill level defined in the unit objective. Programmed learning/instruction is not necessarily related to computer programming, although many effective and creative, interactive, and instructional programs are used with students on computers and computer networks. Rather, it is a program of instruction intended to bring a student who is at a predetermined level of skill or knowledge to the next level with materials appropriate to realize pre-established objectives.

While many approaches to programmed learning have been developed over the years, using a variety of media and incorporating sound pedagogical tenets, they still share common attributes. Generally, they are modular. A module is an instructional package teaching a single conceptual unit of subject matter. It is intended to individualize learning by enabling the student to master one unit of content before moving to another. Larger concepts or topics are broken down into useful and measurable component parts and each part is taught as a module. The modules are logically linked to bring the student, step-by-step, to the point of achieving all the objectives in the course.

When providing instructional support, teaching assistants should employ the concept of teaching through the use of perspective. There is always more than one way to "see" or approach a problem, an example, a process, fact or event, or any learning situation. Varying approaches for instruction helps to maintain the students' interest in the material and can address the diverse needs of individuals to comprehend the material. Opportunities to employ teaching through the use of perspective abound: when drilling on assigned reading exercises; using pictorial or video materials to demonstrate, reinforce or enhance the reading experience; and, particularly, when relating reading materials to real-life contexts that may provide the students with a better comprehension of the materials and help to enable skill acquisition.

Skill 13.2 Helps students use instructional resources (e.g., dictionaries, encyclopedias, multimedia materials) to support reading

Dictionaries are useful for spelling, writing, and reading. It is very important to initially expose and habituate students to enjoy using the dictionary. Cooper (2004) suggests that the following be kept in mind as the teacher of grades K-6 introduces and then habituates children in what is to be hoped will be a lifelong fascination with the dictionary and vocabulary acquisition.

Requesting or suggesting that children look up a word in the dictionary should be an invitation to a wonderful exploration, not a punishment or busy work that has no reference to their current reading assignment.

Model the correct way to use the dictionary for children even as late as the third – sixth grade. Many have never been taught proper dictionary skills. The teacher needs to demonstrate to the children that as an adult reader and writer, he or she routinely and happily uses the dictionary and learns new content that makes him or her better at reading and writing.

Do not routinely require children to look up every new spelling word in the dictionary (this is Cooper's view and many other theorists would disagree with him here).

Cooper believes in beginning dictionary study as early as kindergarten and this is now very possible because of the proliferation of lush picture dictionaries which can be introduced at that grade level. He also suggests that children not only look at these picture dictionaries, but also begin to make dictionaries of their own at this grade level filled with pictures and beginning words. As children join the circle of lexicographers, they will begin to see themselves as compilers and users of dictionaries. Of course, this will support their ongoing vocabulary development.

On early grade levels, use of the dictionary can nicely complement the children's mastery of the alphabet. They should be given whole class and small group practice in locating words.

As the children progress with their phonetic skills, the dictionary can be used to show them phonetic respelling using the pronunciation key.

Older children in grades 3 and beyond need explicit teacher demonstrations and practice in the use of guide words. They also need to begin to learn about the hierarchies of various word meanings. In the upper grades, children should also explore using special content dictionaries and glossaries in the backs of their books.

Key Words

Cooper (2004) feels that it is up to the teacher to preview the content area text to identify the main ideas. Then the teacher should compile a list of terms related to the content. These terms and words become part of the key concepts list.

Next, the teacher sees which of the key concept words and terms are already defined in the text. These will not require direct teaching. Words, for which children have sufficient skills to determine their meaning, through base, root, prefixes or suffixes, also will not require direct teaching.

Instruction in the remaining key words, which should not be more than two or three in number, can be provided before, during or after reading. If students have previewed the content area and identified those words they need support on, the instruction should be provided before reading. Instruction can also easily be provided as part of guided reading support. After-reading support is indicated when the text offers the children an opportunity to enrich their own vocabularies.

Having children work as a whole class or in small groups on a content specific dictionary for a topic regularly covered in their grade level social studies, science, or mathematics curriculum offers an excellent collaborative opportunity for children to design a dictionary/word resource that can celebrate their own vocabulary learning. Such a resource can then be used with the next year's classes as well.

Encyclopedias

At the appropriate age/grade level, students will be introduced to the encyclopedia by the classroom teacher or school librarian as a compendium of knowledge and a principal tool for reference and research. As with all learning tools, students must be made aware of the purposes and processes of using the encyclopedia and the differences from other seemingly similar tools or applications.

For example, when deciding whether the dictionary or the encyclopedia is the appropriate tool for a specific task, students are taught that they are alike by both using alphabetic ordering. They are different in purpose as well as application. The dictionary is used to <u>define</u> the correct spelling, proper meaning and appropriate uses of a word. The encyclopedia is used to succinctly <u>explain</u> a topic. Usually, the encyclopedia is introduced when students are ready to do supplemental reading or begin writing compositions or research papers with prescribed topics.

Teachers or librarians introducing encyclopedia use as a measurable skill will often assign and evaluate practice research projects for students. Examples of these would be:

- Working sequentially through a numbered list of randomly alphabetized sample topics, the student will locate each sample topic in the encyclopedia and cite book and page number(s) for each one.
- Working sequentially through a numbered list of randomly alphabetized sample topics, the student will select related subtopics from another list (or create his or her own list). The student will locate each subtopic in the encyclopedia and cite book and page number(s) for each one.
- Working sequentially through a numbered list of randomly alphabetized sample topics, the student will identify and list valid cross references, locate these within the encyclopedia and cite book and page number(s) for each one.

Multimedia Resources

The impact on today's society by media is immense and ever-increasing. Children watch programs on television that are amazingly fast-paced and visually rich. Parent's roles as verbal and moral teachers are diminishing in response to the much more stimulating guidance of the television set. Adolescence, which used to be the time for going out and exploring the world first hand, is now consumed by the allure of MTV, popular music, and video games. Young adults are exposed to uncensored sex and violence.

But the effect of media on society is beneficial and progressive at the same time. Its effect on education in particular provides special challenges and opportunities for teachers and students.

Thanks to satellite technology, instructional radio and television programs can be received by urban classrooms and rural villages. CD-roms can allow students to learn information through a virtual reality experience. The Internet allows instant access to unlimited data and connects people across all cultures through shared interests. Educational media, when used in a productive way, enriches instruction and makes it more individualized, accessible, and economical.

One of the most interesting ways in which the web complements the Reading and Writing Workshop involves the proliferation of author specific web resources. If used judiciously, these web resources allow authors to "come into" the classroom and allow children to write, question, discuss and share their literacy experiences with the authors themselves. Children can also readily become part of a distanced community of peers who are also reading works by a given author.

For instance, children who have been introduced to the work of Faith Ringgold, the author of *Tar Beach*, can easily visit her online site, www.faithringgold.com. Here they will not only find extensive biographic data on Faith, but they will also be able to learn a song inspired by her main character Cassie. They will be able to help illustrate a new story Faith has put up on the website, and also see if any of the questions they may have generated in their shared or independent reading of her books has already been answered in the FAQ-frequently asked questions section of her web resource. Most of the author websites respond online to individual children's questions.

There are even some reader response web resources such as the spaghetti review web site where young readers can post their response to different books they are reading. http://www.book-club-review.com/view.php?cid=1

Skill 13.3 **Helps students use a variety of approaches to understand what they read (e.g., skimming, questioning to tap prior knowledge, monitoring understanding, reviewing, summarizing)**

As children progress to the older grades (3-6), it is important for the teacher to model for them that in research on a social studies or science exploration, it may not be necessary to read every single word of a given expository information text. For instance, if the child is trying to find out about hieroglyphics, he or she might only read through those sections of a book on Egyptian or Sumerian civilization which dealt with picture writing. The teacher, assisted by a child, should model how to go through the table of contents and the index of the book to identify only those pages which deal with picture writing. In addition, other children should come to the front of the room or to the center of the area where the reading group is meeting. They should then with the support of the teacher skim through the book for illustrations or diagrams of picture writing which is the focus of their need.

Children can practice the skills of skimming texts and scanning for particular topics that connect with their grade level social studies, science and mathematics content area interests.

Certainly children need to understand and to be comfortable with the fact that not every single expository text is meant to be read thoroughly and completely.

Comprehension Skills

Cooper (2004) advocates that the child ask himself or herself what a text is about before he or she reads it and even as he or she is in the process of reading the text, that he or she note what he or she thinks the text is going to be about. While the child is reading the text, Cooper (2004) feels that the child should be continually questioning himself or herself as to whether the text confirmed the child's predictions. Of course after completing the text, the child can then review the predictions and verify whether they were correct.

Again within the framework set by Cooper in his *Literacy: Helping Children Construct Meaning*, the child reader looks over the expository text subheads, illustrations, captions and indices to get an idea about the text. Then the child, still before reading the text, decides that perhaps he or she can find the answer to questions he or she has generated.

During the reading, the child is asking himself or herself, "Am I finding the answer to my question?"

After the reading, the child notes: I have found the answer to my question. This book or electronic text is an excellent source of information for me about my question. (Or perhaps, No, I have not found the answer to my question. This book or electronic text is not a good source of information for me about my question. I will have to look for other resources).

Role of oral language fluency

Children on the middle and secondary levels of education who are studying social studies content, have been exposed to what social studies educators call re-enactments. This is a reader's theater format based completely on fact and established historical texts and documents: an authentic version of history and cultural study.

Even young children will enjoy and gain tremendous additional expository comprehension facility when they are asked to dramatize a well known historical document or song: In "acting" out the preamble to the Constitution or reading aloud as a chorus the Declaration of Independence or in dramatizing the "Battle Hymn of the Republic," children have to examine in a deep form the vocabulary, syntactic, and semantic clues of these texts. They then have to use their oral instruments (voices) to impart the intended expression to the texts.

If the children are in grades 4 and above, they can also be asked to "explain" in writing how they used the word, syntactic and semantic clues to style their oral language recitation. The recitation and writing can be a powerful experience for children grades 4 and up as they build their expository reading and writing skills.

Strategies for Improving Comprehension

Retelling

Retelling needs to be very clearly defined so that the child reader does not think that the teacher wants him or her to spill the WHOLE story back in the retelling. A child should be able to talk comfortably and fluently about the story he or she has just read. He or she should be able to tell the main things that have happened in the story.

When a child retells a story to a teacher, the teacher needs ways to help him or her assess the child's understanding. Ironically, the teacher can use some of the same strategies he or she suggests to the child to assess the child's understanding of a book which is not familiar to the teacher. These strategies include: back cover reading, scanning the table of contents, looking at the pictures, and reading the book jacket.

If the child can explain how the story turned out and provide examples to support these explanations, try not to interrupt him or her with too many questions.

Children can use the text of the book to reinforce what they are saying, and they can even read from it if they wish. It is also important to note that some children need to re-read the text twice and their re-reading of it is out of enjoyment.
I
When the teacher plans to use the retelling as a way of assessing the child, then the following ground rules have to be set and made clear to the child.

The teacher explains the purpose of the retelling to determine how well the child is reading at the outset of the conference.

The teacher maintains in the child's assessment notebook or in his/her assessment record what the child is saying in phrases, not sentences. Just enough is recorded to indicate whether the child actually understood the story. The teacher also tries to analyze from the retelling if the child cannot comprehend a given text. If the child's accuracy rate with the text is below 95 per cent, then the problem is at the word level, but the accuracy rate for the text is above 95 per cent, the difficulty lies at the text level.

Inferencing

Inferencing is an evaluative process that involves the reader making a reasonable judgment based on the information given and engages children in literally constructing meaning. In order to develop and enhance this key skill in children, they might have a mini lesson where the teacher demonstrates this key skill by reading an expository book aloud (i.e. one on skyscrapers for young children) and then demonstrates for them the following reading habits: looking for clues, reflecting on what the reader already knows about the topic ("activating prior knowledge"), and using the clues in the expository text to figure out what the author means/intends.

Main Idea

Identifying main ideas in an expository text can be improved when the children have an explicit strategy for identifying important information. They can be make this strategy part of their everyday reading style by being focused and "walked" through the following exercises as a part of a series of guided reading sessions. The child should read the passage so that the topic is readily identifiable to him or her. It will be what most of the information is about.

Next the child should be asked to be on the lookout for a sentence within the expository passage that summarizes the key information in the paragraph or in the lengthier excerpt. Then the child should read the rest of the passage or excerpt in light of this information and also note which information in the paragraph is not important. The important information the child has identified in the paragraph can be used by the child reader to formulate the author's main idea. The child reader may even want to use some of the author's own language in formulating that idea.

Monitoring

Monitoring means self-clarifying: As a reader reads, the reader often realizes that what he or she is reading is not making sense. The reader then has to have a plan for making sensible meaning out of the excerpt. Cooper and other balanced literacy advocates have a stop-and-think strategy which they use with children. The child reflects, "Does this make sense to me?" When the child concludes that it does not, the child then either: re-reads, reads ahead in the text, looks up unknown words, or asks for help from the teacher.

What is important about monitoring is that some readers ask these questions and try these approaches without ever being explicitly taught them in school by a teacher. However, these strategies need to be explicitly modeled and practiced under the guidance of the teacher by most, if not all child readers.

ATAS

Summarizing

Summarizing engages the reader in pulling together into a cohesive whole, the essential bits of information within a longer passage or excerpt of text. Children can be taught to summarize informational or expository text by following these guidelines. First they should look at the topic sentence of the paragraph or the text and delete the trivia. Then they should search for information which has been mentioned more than once and make sure it is included only once in their summary. Then find related ideas or items and group them under a unifying heading. Search for and identify a main idea sentence. Put the summary together using all these guidelines.

Questions

Generating questions can motivate and enhance children's comprehension of reading in that they are actively involved in generating their own questions and then answer these questions based on their reading. The following guidelines will help children generate meaningful questions that will trigger constructive reading of expository texts. First children should preview the text by reading the titles and subheads. Then they should also look at the illustrations and the pictures. Finally they should read the first paragraph. These first previews should yield an impressive batch of specific questions.

Next, children should get into their Dr. Seuss mode and ask themselves a "THINK" question. For younger children, having a "THINK" silly hat in the classroom as an idea might be effective as well, so that the children could actually go over and put it on. Make certain that the children write down the question. Then have them read to find important information to answer their "Think" question. Ask that they write down the answer they found and copy the sentence or sentences where they found the answer. Also have them consider whether, in light of their further reading through the text, their original question was a good one or not.

Ask them to be prepared to explain why their original question was a good one or not. Once the children have answered their original "think" question, have them generate additional ones and then find their answers and judge whether these questions were "good" ones in light of the text.

Skill 13.4 Gathers information about students' progress as readers to support the teacher's planning, assessment, and instruction

Depending on the classroom teacher's specific methods and processes for planning, delivering and evaluating instruction, effective support can be provided in correlating test results, prompting and quizzing individuals and groups regarding specified reading skills (as requested by the teacher) and identifying and documenting strengths and weaknesses. Interacting with students can also identify those who are reading well above or well below the assigned level, as well as those who are struggling to maintain reading ability at the assigned level.

Working with individuals, it should be possible to identify any problems with character recognition, phonetic skill, word and phrase comprehension. All of these would be noted and reported to the classroom teacher. Evidence of undiagnosed dyslexia should always be reported to the teacher.

TEACHER CERTIFICATION STUDY GUIDE

COMPETENCY 14.0 UNDERSTANDS CLASSROOM INSTRUCTION RELATED TO WRITING

Skill 14.1 Understands drafting, editing, and proofreading written work

Writing is a recursive process. As students engage in the various stages of writing, they develop and improve not only their writing skills, but their thinking skills as well. Students must understand that writing is a process that typically involves many steps when writing quality work. No matter the level of writer, students should be experienced in the following stages of the writing process. The stages of the writing process are as follows:

Prewriting

Students gather ideas before writing. Prewriting may include clustering, listing, brainstorming, mapping, free writing, and charting. Providing many ways for a student to develop ideas on a topic will increase his/her chances for success.

Remind students that as they prewrite, they need to consider their audience. Prewriting strategies assist students in a variety of ways. Listed below are the most common prewriting strategies students can use to explore, plan and write on a topic. It is important to remember when teaching these strategies that not all prewriting must eventually produce a finished piece of writing. In fact, in the initial lesson of teaching prewriting strategies, it might be more effective to have students practice prewriting strategies without the pressure of having to write a finished product.

- Keep an idea book so that they can jot down ideas that come to mind
- Write in a daily journal
- Write down whatever comes to mind; this is called free writing. Students do not stop to make corrections or interrupt the flow of ideas.

A variation of this technique is focused free writing - writing on a specific topic - to prepare for an essay.

- Make a list of all ideas connected with their topic; this is called brainstorming
- Make sure students know that this technique works best when they let their mind work freely. After completing the list, students should analyze the list to see if a pattern or way to group the ideas
- Ask the questions Who? What? When? Where? When? and How? Help the writer approach a topic from several perspectives
- Create a visual map on paper to gather ideas. Cluster circles and lines to show connections between ideas. Students should try to identify the relationship that exists between and among their ideas. If they cannot see the relationships, have them pair up, exchange papers and have their partners look for some related ideas
- Observe details of sight, hearing, taste, touch, and taste
- Visualize by making mental images of something and write down the details in a list

After students have practiced with each of these prewriting strategies, ask them to pick out the ones they prefer and ask them to discuss how they might use the techniques to help them with future writing assignments. It is important to remember that they can use more than one prewriting strategy at a time. Also they may find that different writing situations may call for certain techniques.

Drafting

Students compose the first draft. Students should follow their notes/writing plan from the prewriting stage.

Revision and Editing

Revise comes from the Latin word *revidere*, meaning, "to see again." Revision is probably the most important step for the writer in the writing process. Here, students examine their work and make changes in sentences, wording, details and ideas. So many times, students write a draft and then feel they're done. On the contrary – students must be encouraged to develop, change, and enhance their writing as they go, as well as once they've completed a draft.

Therefore, effective teachers realize that revision and editing go hand-in-hand and that students often move back and forth between these stages during the course of one written work. Also, these stages must be practiced in small groups, pairs and/or individually. Students must learn to analyze and improve their own work as well as the works of their peers. Some methods to use include:

1. Students, working in pairs, analyze sentences for variety.
2. Students work in pairs or groups to ask questions about unclear areas in the writing or to help students add details, information, etc.
3. Students perform a final edit.

Many teachers introduce Writer's Workshop to their students to maximize learning about the writing process. Writer's Workshops vary across classrooms, but the main idea is for students to become comfortable with the writing process to produce written work. A basic Writer's Workshop will include a block of classroom time committed to writing various projects (i.e., narratives, memoirs, book summaries, fiction, book reports, etc). Students use this time to write, meet with others to review/edit writing, make comments on writing, revise their own work, proofread, meet with the teacher, and publish their work.

Teachers who facilitate effective Writer's Workshops are able to meet with students one at a time and can guide that student in their individual writing needs. This approach allows the teacher to differentiate instruction for each student's writing level.

Students need to be trained to become effective at proofreading, revising and editing strategies. Begin by training them using both desk-side and scheduled conferences. Listed below are some strategies to use to guide students through the final stages of the writing process (and these can easily be incorporated into Writer's Workshop).

- Provide some guide sheets or forms for students to use while giving peer responses
- Allow students to work in pairs and limit the agenda
- Model the use of the guide sheet or form for the entire class
- Give students a time limit or number of written pieces to be completed in a specific amount of time
- Have the students read their partners' papers and ask at least three who, what, when, why, how questions. The students answer the questions and use them as a place to begin discussing the piece
- At this point in the writing process a mini-lesson that focuses on some of the problems your students are having would be appropriate

To help students revise, provide students with a series of questions that will assist them in revising their writing

1. Do the details give a clear picture? Add details that appeal to more than just the sense of sight.

2. How effectively are the details organized? Reorder the details if it is needed.

3. Are the thoughts and feelings of the writer included? Add personal thoughts and feelings about the subject.

As you discuss revision, you begin with discussing the definition of revise. Also, state that all writing must be revised to improve it. After students have revised their writing, it is time for the final editing and proofreading.

Proofreading

Students proofread the draft for punctuation and mechanical errors. There are a few key points to remember when helping students learn to edit and proofread their work.

- It is crucial that students are not taught grammar in isolation, but in the context of the writing process
- Ask students to read their writing and check for specific errors such as using a subordinate clause as a sentence
- Provide students with a proofreading checklist to guide them as they edit their work

Publishing

Students may have their work displayed on a bulletin board, read aloud in class, or printed in a literary magazine or school anthology.

It is important to realize that these steps are recursive; as a student engages in each aspect of the writing process, he or she may begin with prewriting, write, revise, write, revise, edit, and publish. They do not engage in this process in a lockstep manner; it is more circular.

TEACHER CERTIFICATION STUDY GUIDE

Teacher Assessment

When assessing and responding to student writing, there are several guidelines to remember.

- Use a rating system. For example, a scale from 1 to 4 (where 1=unsatisfactory and 4=excellent).
- Monitor their use of source material
- Evaluate the structure and development of students' writing
- Ensure that their writing style is appropriate for the task assigned
- Check for grammatical correctness
- Provide follow-up support for any weaknesses detected

Below are a few more tips for assessing students' writing:

Responding to non-graded writing (formative)
1. Avoid using a red pen. Whenever possible use a #2 pencil.
2. Explain the criteria that will be used for assessment in advance.
3. Read the writing once while asking the question, "Is the student's response appropriate for the assignment?"
4. Reread and make note at the end whether the student met the objective of the writing task.
5. Responses should be non-critical and use supportive and encouraging language.
6. Resist writing on or over the student's writing.
7. Highlight the ideas you wish to emphasize, question, or verify.
8. Encourage your students to take risks.

Responding to and evaluating graded writing (summative)
1. Ask students to submit prewriting and rough-draft materials including all revisions with their final draft.
2. For the first reading, use a holistic method, examining the work as a whole.
3. When reading the draft for the second time, assess it using the standards previously established.
4. Responses to the writing should be written in the margin and should use supportive language.
5. Make sure you address the process as well as the product. It is important that students value the learning process as well as the final product.
6. After scanning the piece a third time, write final comments at the end of the draft.

Skill 14.2 Helps students focus their writing

Focus is a significant aspect of a written work. Writing must be focused so as to retain the reader's interests, as well as ensure the reader can follow the writing. Below are some strategies to help students to focus written work:

Enhancing Interest

- Start out with an attention-grabbing introduction. This sets an engaging tone for the entire piece and will be more likely to pull the reader in.
- Use dynamic vocabulary and varied sentence beginnings. Keep the readers on their toes. If they can predict what you are going to say next, switch it up.
- Avoid using clichés (as cold as ice, the best thing since sliced bread, nip it in the bud). These are easy shortcuts, but they are not interesting, memorable, or convincing.

Ensuring Understanding

- Avoid using the words, "clearly," "obviously," and "undoubtedly." Often, things that are clear or obvious to the author are not as apparent to the reader. Instead of using these words, make your point so strongly that it is clear on its own.
- Use the word that best fits the meaning you intend for, even if it is longer or a little less common. Try to find a balance, and sometimes go with a familiar yet precise word.
- When in doubt, explain further.

Skill 14.3 Helps students use instructional resources (e.g., dictionaries, grammar books, library resources, technological resources) to support writing

It is necessary for each student to become knowledgeable about, and comfortable with using, all instructional resources. But the primary skill each student must acquire is the ability to identify their assignment's specific problem, issue or need to be addressed. If this can be understood and verbalized, then the student will be able to select the appropriate resource tool from among the available resources, once these have been introduced, used and understood.

As early as possible, we try to instill the skills necessary to make each child an independent researcher. The teaching faculty and library and support staff should work together to ensure that all students know the location of, and have access to, all appropriate learning resources, whether in the classroom, the school library, a lab or other resource center. The students should be made familiar with the layout of each resource center and understand the operations of available equipment. This could be anything from a card catalogue to a computer terminal or microfilm reader.

Working with each student to associate appropriate resources with identifiable needs is primary. Teaching effective and efficient use of each resource is the next concern. Time and practice (preferably, with prescribed exercises) should be expended on the rudiments of using explicit directives (such as tables of contents, indices, or Web browsers) to make a necessary search expeditious, effective and even fun. Repeated and purposeful practice is the surest method of instilling these skills in young students. Children are sometimes impulsive and impatient. Even after students have been taught proper reference and research procedure and technique, many will choose to just jump right into the text and slog back and forth through the pages, randomly, seeking an answer.

While it can never be by nature instinctive, it should become second nature for the student (through practice) to always reference a table of contents and/or index to expedite the search, avoid frustration and make the task easier.

Skill 14.4 Gathers information about students' progress as writers to support the teacher's planning, assessment, and instruction

One of the increasingly popular and meaningful forms of informal assessment is the compilation of the literacy portfolio. What is particularly compelling about this type of informal portfolio is that artists, television directors, authors, architects and photographers use portfolios in their careers and jobs. This is a most authentic format for documenting children's literacy growth over time. The portfolio is not only a significant professional informal assessment tool for the teacher; but a vehicle and format for the child reader to take ownership of his or her progress over time as a reader and writer. It models a way of compiling one's reading and writing products as a lifelong learner, which is the ultimate goal of reading instruction.

Portfolios should include the following six categories of materials:

Work samples- These can include children's story maps, webs, K-W-L charts, pictures, illustrations, storyboards, and writings about the stories which they have read.

Records of Independent Reading and Writing—These can include the children's journals, notebooks or logs of books reads with the names of the authors, titles of the books, date completed, and pieces related to that book completed or in progress.

Checklists and Surveys- These include checklists designed by the teacher for reading development, writing development, ownership check lists, and general interest surveys.

Self Evaluation Forms- These are the children's own evaluations of their reading and writing process framed in their own words. They can be simple templates with starting sentences such as: "I am really proud of the way I ...

I feel one of my strengths as a reader is _____

To improve the way I read aloud I need to _____

To improve my reading I should _____

Some teachers and schools also advocate having the child include formal test results and questions within the portfolio.

Generally at the beginning of a child's portfolio in grade 3 or above there is a letter to the reader explaining the work that will be found in the portfolio and from fourth grade level up, children write a brief reflection detailing their feelings and judgments about their growth as readers and writers.

When teachers are maintaining the portfolios for mandated school administrative review, district review, or even for their own research, they often prepare portfolio summary sheets which provide identifying data on the children and then a timeline of their review of the portfolio contents and their professional comments on the extent to which the portfolio documents satisfactory and ongoing growth in reading, say in constructing meaning, self-evaluation, oral fluency, and the like.

Portfolios can be used beneficially for child-teacher and of course, parent/teacher conversations to:

- Review the child's progress.
- Discuss area of strength.
- Set Future Goals
- Make plans for future learning activities and
- Evaluate what should remain in the portfolio and what needs to be cleared out for new material.

Rubrics

Holistic scoring involves assessing a child's ability to construct meaning through writing. It uses a scale called a RUBRIC which ranges from 0 to 4.

O- Would be for a piece which can not be scored. It does not respond to the topic asked or is illegible.

1- Would be a writing which does respond to the topic, but does not cover it accurately.

2- Would be for a response which is on the questions, but lacks sufficient details to convey the purpose and to accomplish the writing task requested.

3- Would be a paper which in general fulfills the purpose of the writing assignment and demonstrates that the reader correctly constructed meaning. The reader showed that he or she understands the writer's purpose and message.

4- This response has the most details, best organization, and presents a well expressed reaction to the original writer's piece.

Miscue Analysis

This is a procedure that allows the teacher a look at the student's reading process individually. By definition, the miscue is an oral response different from the text being read. Sometimes miscues are also called unexpected responses or errors. By studying a student's miscues from an oral reading sample, the teacher can determine which cues and strategies the student is correctly using or not using in constructing meaning. Of course, the teacher can customize instruction to meet the needs of this particular student.

Informal Reading Inventories (IRI)

These are a series of samples of texts prearranged in stages of increasing difficulty. Listening to children read through these inventories, the teacher can pinpoint their level and the additional inventories they need to work on.

Group versus Individual Reading Assessments

Part of the successful teaching of reading is the organizational strategy of using flexible groups in contrast to whole class and individual activities. Flexible groups may consist of two, three, or more students working together to accomplish a specific purpose.

This is in contrast to the more traditional purpose of reading groups where children were assigned or "tracked" for a long period of time (often for the entire school year). The flexible reading groups suggested here are convened together for a specific purpose and can last for a few days or may be changed every day.

The size of the group is closely aligned to the purpose as well. Teachers do not really have hard and fast rules to follow with these groups, but the rule of thumb in terms of numbers of children within each type of flexible group is to keep the group small enough so that it can accomplish its purpose.

Interest groups have children with the same interest work together to create a demonstration, experiment, reading, or presentation with charts and other resources. This can also be used for collaborative writing or shared writing.

Strengths /needs groups happen when children with common strengths and needs are deliberately grouped together. This works well for a mini lesson or for a discussion.

COMPETENCY 15.0 UNDERSTANDS CLASSROOM INSTRUCTION RELATED TO MATHEMATICS

Skill 15.1 Relates mathematics to everyday situations

Teachers can increase student interest in math and promote learning and understanding by relating mathematical concepts to the lives of students. Instead of using only abstract presentations and examples, teachers should relate concepts to real-world situations to shift the emphasis from memorization and abstract application to understanding and applied problem solving. In addition, relating math to careers and professions helps illustrate the relevance of math and aids in the career exploration process.

Mathematics is an important part of the everyday lives of students. Instructors should, as discussed in previous sections, expose students to math problems involving money, recipes, time keeping, sports, or other areas of interest. Such real-world problems stimulate student interest and promote understanding.

As another example, when teaching a unit on the geometry of certain shapes, teachers can ask students to design a structure of interest to the student using the shapes in question. This exercise serves the dual purpose of teaching students to learn and apply the properties (e.g. area, volume) of shapes while demonstrating the relevance of geometry to architectural and engineering professions.

Skill 15.2 Identifies and corrects basic errors in addition, subtraction, multiplication, and division

Addition Errors

Common errors in elementary column addition include failing to "carry" to the next column and failing to properly align numbers for column addition.

Examples:

1. $\begin{array}{r} 19 \\ +17 \\ \hline 26 \end{array}$

2. $\begin{array}{r} 84 \\ 7 \\ +156 \\ \hline 310 \end{array}$

Solutions:

1. In this basic addition problem, the student failed to carry the 1 from the addition of 9 and 7 in the ones' place. Thus, her answer was off by 10. The correct answer is 36.

2. In this problem, the student failed to properly align the 7 for column addition. Instead, she added the 7 as if it were 70. Thus, her answer was off by 63 (70-7). The correct answer is 247.

TEACHER CERTIFICATION STUDY GUIDE

Subtraction Errors

Common errors in elementary column subtraction include failing to "borrow" and borrowing improperly.

Examples:
1.   57
    - 19
     42

2.   2(13)(15)
    4̶3̶5̶
   - 178
    167

3.   4(10)(13)
    5̶0̶3̶
   - 267
    246

4.   9(13)
    5̶0̶3̶
   - 267
    336

Solutions:

1. In this problem, the student failed to borrow and instead subtracted the smaller number from the larger number regardless of position. The correct answer is 38.

2. In this problem, the student borrowed incorrectly. He simply took two from the hundreds' column and gave one to both the ones' and tens' column. The correct answer is 257.

3. In this problem, the student borrowed incorrectly. While he did change the 0 to 10 after borrowing from the hundreds' place; he failed to decrease the 10 to 9 when borrowing for the ones' place. The correct answer is 236.

4. In this problem, the student borrowed incorrectly. While he properly changed the 0 to 9 when borrowing, he failed to borrow from the hundreds' place. He should have reduced the 5 to 4. The correct answer is 236.

Multiplication Errors

Common errors in elementary multiplication include failing to follow the proper sequence in column multiplication, failing to insert a zero in the second row of two-digit multiplication, and improperly handling carried numbers.

Examples:

1. $\overset{1}{}45$
    $\underline{\times3}$
    155

2. 234
    $\underline{\times 112}$
    238

3. 152
    $\underline{\times13}$
    456
    $\underline{152}$
    608

4. $\overset{5}{}27$
    $\underline{\times8}$
    806

Solutions:

1. In this problem, the student did not properly handle the carried number. Instead of adding 1 to the product of 4 and 3, she multiplied both 4 and 1 by 3 and added the result. The correct answer is 135.

2. In this problem, the student did not follow the proper sequence. She simply multiplied straight down each column, as in addition or subtraction. The correct answer is 26,208.

3. In this problem, the student failed to add a zero to the end of the tens' column product. The correct answer is 1976.

4. In this problem, the student did not properly handle the carried number. She multiplied the product by the carried number instead of adding the carried number. The correct answer is 216.

TEACHER CERTIFICATION STUDY GUIDE

Division Errors

Because long division involves many operations and complex sequences, there is great potential for error. Common long division errors include placing numbers in the wrong locations, making errors in subtraction or multiplication, and failing to properly "bring down" the next number after subtraction.

Examples:

1. $\begin{array}{r} 28 \\ 7{\overline{\smash{)}149}} \\ \underline{-\ 9} \\ 59 \\ \underline{-56} \\ 3 \end{array}$
2. $\begin{array}{r} 2 \\ 7{\overline{\smash{)}149}} \\ \underline{-14} \\ 135 \end{array}$
3. $\begin{array}{r} 20 \\ 7{\overline{\smash{)}149}} \\ \underline{-14} \\ 0 \end{array}$
4. $\begin{array}{r} 21 \\ 7{\overline{\smash{)}149}} \\ \underline{-14} \\ 09 \\ \underline{-7} \\ 2 \end{array}$

Solutions:

1. In this problem, the student added when he should have multiplied (i.e. 2 + 7 instead of 2 x 7).

2. In this problem, the student subtracted incorrectly. He placed the product of 2 and 7 in the wrong location.

3. In this problem, the student failed to bring down the 9 following subtraction.

4. The student worked this problem correctly.

Skill 15.3 Helps students use instructional resources (e.g., hands-on materials, rulers, money, charts, graphs, technological resources) to support mathematical learning

Graphs

To make a **bar graph** or a **pictograph**, determine the scale to be used for the graph. Then determine the length of each bar on the graph or determine the number of pictures needed to represent each item of information. Be sure to include an explanation of the scale in the legend.

Example: A class had the following grades:

4 A's, 9 B's, 8 C's, 1 D, 3 F's.

Graph these on a bar graph and a pictograph.

Pictograph

Grade	Number of Students
A	☺☺☺☺
B	☺☺☺☺☺☺☺☺☺
C	☺☺☺☺☺☺☺☺
D	☺
F	☺☺☺

Bar graph

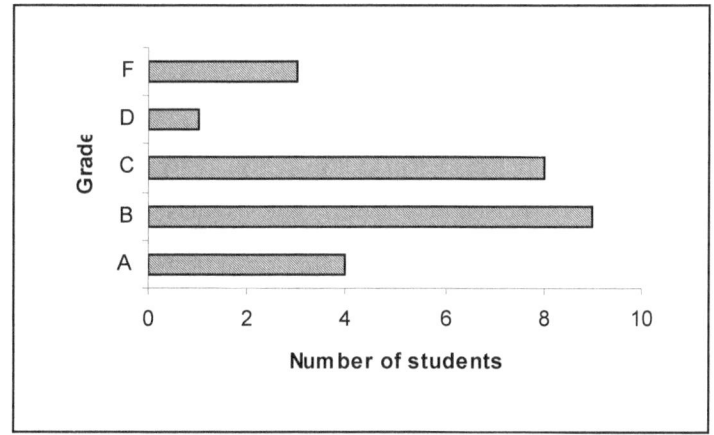

To make a **line graph**, determine appropriate scales for both the vertical and horizontal axes (based on the information to be graphed). Describe what each axis represents and mark the scale periodically on each axis. Graph the individual points of the graph and connect the points on the graph from left to right.

Example: Graph the following information using a line graph.

The number of National Merit finalists/school year

	90-'91	91-'92	92-'93	93-'94	94-'95	95-'96
Central	3	5	1	4	6	8
Wilson	4	2	3	2	3	2

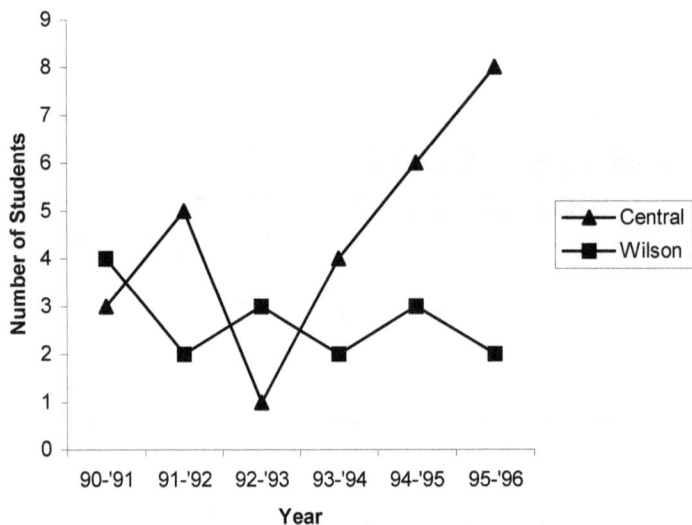

To make a **circle graph**, total all the information that is to be included on the graph. Determine the central angle to be used for each sector of the graph using the following formula:

$$\frac{\text{information}}{\text{total information}} \times 360° = \text{degrees in central } \sphericalangle$$

Lay out the central angles to these sizes, label each section and include its percent.

Example: Graph this information on a circle graph:

Monthly expenses:

  Rent, $400
  Food, $150
  Utilities, $75
  Clothes, $75
  Church, $100
  Misc., $200

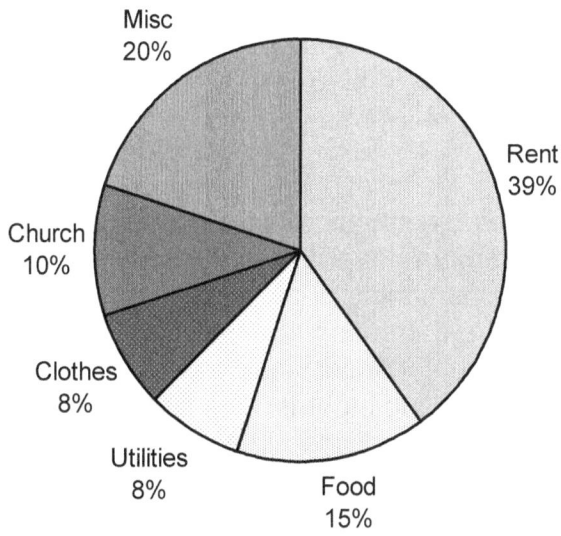

To read a bar graph or a pictograph, read the explanation of the scale that was used in the legend. Compare the length of each bar with the dimensions on the axes and calculate the value each bar represents. On a pictograph count the number of pictures used in the chart and calculate the value of all the pictures.

To read a circle graph, find the total of the amounts represented on the entire circle graph. To determine the actual amount that each sector of the graph represents, multiply the percent in a sector times the total amount number.

To read a chart read the row and column headings on the table. Use this information to evaluate the given information in the chart.

Hands-on Materials
Manipulatives are hands-on objects that are useful to mathematics teachers. Two common types of manipulatives are blocks and tiles that students use to conceptualize arithmetic problems and figures that students use to explore geometric problems.

Base ten blocks and tiles help students explore the concept of place value and arithmetic operations. Blocks of different colors and sizes represent different place values (e.g. ones, tens, hundreds). Students can physically manipulate the blocks to solve arithmetic problems. For example, students add or take away blocks to solve addition and subtraction problems, and group blocks to solve division problems.

Manipulatives of different geometric shapes help students explore geometric properties. For example, students can use tangrams to make different shapes and solve interesting and challenging puzzles.

Rulers
Math students use rulers to measure objects. Instructors should teach students to read both metric and standard rulers. In general, we measure an object by placing the left-hand, zero end at the beginning of the object and extending the ruler along the length of the object. We determine the length by reading the measurement on the ruler where the object ends. The basic units of standard rulers are inches, with each inch divided into eighths. The basic units of metric rulers are centimeters, with each centimeter divided into ten millimeters.

Money
Money is an important topic in elementary math classes. Students learn to count, add, subtract, and convert money. The use of actual money to solve problems helps students conceptualize the processes. In addition, teachers can use coins as generic objects to help students understand processes like division. For example, a teacher may ask his students to divide a bag of pennies into a certain number of groups.

Charts
Examples of charts of interest to math teachers are basic number charts and operation charts. Teachers can use charts of multiplication tables to help teach multiplication by drilling. In addition, students can use such charts to help them complete problems while they are in the process of memorizing multiplication tables. Teachers can use basic number charts (e.g. a chart with the numbers 1 to 100) to help make abstract ideas more concrete. For example, a teacher may ask her students to highlight a number chart by 3's. This exercise helps students understand the concept of counting by 3's and repeated addition of 3's.

TEACHER CERTIFICATION STUDY GUIDE

Technological Resources

Calculators and computers are two important technological tools of use to the math teacher and student. Because calculators are almost necessary in the study of higher math, elementary teachers should introduce students to the basic uses of calculators. Computers also provide many resources for math teachers and students. Teachers and students can use interactive tools and programs on the Internet to further learning of math concepts. In addition, teachers can allow students to explore video games that provide instruction and practice of different types of math problems. Such games provide an entertaining alternative to traditional teaching methods.

Skill 15.4   Gathers information about students' progress in mathematics to support the teacher's planning, assessment, and instruction

Student assessment is an important part of the educational process. High quality assessment methods are necessary for the development and maintenance of a successful learning environment. Teachers must develop and implement assessment procedures that accurately evaluate student progress, test content areas of greatest importance, and enhance and improve learning. To enhance learning and accurately evaluate student progress, teachers should use a variety of assessment tasks to gain a better understanding a student's strengths and weaknesses. Finally, teachers should implement scoring patterns that fairly and accurately evaluate student performance.

Teachers should use a variety of assessment procedures to evaluate student knowledge and understanding. One type of alternative assessment is bundled testing. Bundled testing is the grouping of different question formats for the same skill or competency. For example, a bundled test of exponential functions may include multiple choice questions, short response questions, word problems, and essay questions. The variety of questions tests different levels of reasoning and expression. Another type of alternative assessment is projects. Projects are longer term, creative tasks that require many levels of reasoning and expression. Projects are often a good indicator of understanding because they require high-level thinking. A final type of alternative assessment is student portfolios. Portfolios are collections of student work over a period of time. Portfolios aid in the evaluation of student growth and progress.

Scoring methods are an important, and an often overlooked, part of effective assessment. Teachers can use a simple three-point scale for evaluating student responses. No answer or an inappropriate answer that shows no understanding scores zero points. A partial response showing a lack of understanding, a lack of explanation, or major computational errors scores one point. A somewhat satisfactory answer that answers most of the question correctly but contains simple computational errors or minor flaws in reasoning receives two points. Finally, a satisfactory response displaying full understanding, adequate explanation, and appropriate reasoning receives three points. When evaluating student responses, teachers should look for common error patterns and mistakes in computation. Teachers should also incorporate questions and scoring procedures that address common error patterns and misconceptions into their methods of assessment.

The primary purpose of student assessment is to evaluate the effectiveness of the curriculum and instruction by measuring student performance. Teachers and school officials use the results of student assessments to monitor student progress and modify and design curriculum to meet the needs of the students. Teachers and school officials carefully assess the results of tests to determine the parts of the curriculum that need altering. For example, the results of a test may indicate that the majority of the students in a class struggle with problems involving logarithmic functions. In response to such findings, the teacher would evaluate the method of logarithmic function instruction and make the necessary changes to increase student understanding.

Sample Test

1. $\left(\dfrac{-4}{9}\right) + \left(\dfrac{-7}{10}\right) =$
   (Easy) (Skill 12.2)

   A. $\dfrac{23}{90}$

   B. $\dfrac{-23}{90}$

   C. $\dfrac{103}{90}$

   D. $\dfrac{-103}{90}$

2. $(5.6) \times (-0.11) =$
   (Rigorous) (Skill 12.2)

   A. -0.616

   B. 0.616

   C. -6.110

   D. 6.110

3. $4\dfrac{2}{9} \times \dfrac{7}{10}$
   (Average Rigor) (Skill 12.1)

   A. $4\dfrac{9}{10}$

   B. $\dfrac{266}{90}$

   C. $2\dfrac{43}{45}$

   D. $2\dfrac{6}{20}$

4. $0.74 =$
   (Average Rigor) (Skill 12.2, 12.4)

   A. $\dfrac{74}{100}$

   B. 7.4%

   C. $\dfrac{33}{50}$

   D. $\dfrac{74}{10}$

5. 303 is what percent of 600?
   (Rigorous) (Skill 12.3)

   A. 0.505%

   B. 5.05%

   C. 505%

   D. 50.5%

6. An item that sells for $375 is put on sale at $120. What is the percent of decrease?
   Rigorous) (Skill 12.3)

   A. 25%

   B. 28%

   C. 68%

   D. 34%

7. Two mathematics classes have a total of 410 students. The 8:00 am class has 40 more than the 10:00 am class. How many students are in the 10:00 am class?
(Rigorous) (Skill 12.3)

   A.   123.3

   B.   370

   C.   185

   D.   330

8. A restaurant employs 465 people. There are 280 waiters and 185 cooks. If 168 waiters and 85 cooks receive pay raises, what percent of the waiters will receive a pay raise?
(Rigorous) (Skill 12.3)

   A.   36.13%

   B.   60%

   C.   60.22%

   D.   40%

9. Round $1\frac{13}{16}$ of an inch to the nearest quarter of an inch.
(Rigorous) (Skill 12.1, 12.4)

   A. $1\frac{1}{4}$ inch

   B. $1\frac{5}{8}$ inch

   C. $1\frac{3}{4}$ inch

   D.   2 inches

10. What unit of measurement could we use to report the distance traveled walking around a track?
(Easy) (Skill 9.3)

   A.   degrees

   B.   square meters

   C.   kilometers

   D.   cubic feet

11. $\frac{7}{9} + \frac{1}{3} \div \frac{2}{3} =$
(Easy) (Skill 12.1)

   A. $\frac{5}{3}$

   B. $\frac{3}{2}$

   C.   2

   D. $\frac{23}{18}$

12. Choose the equation that is equivalent to the following:
    (Rigorous) (Skill 12.4)

    $$\frac{3x}{5} - 5 = 5x$$

    A. $3x - 25 = 25x$

    B. $x - \frac{25}{3} = 25x$

    C. $6x - 50 = 75x$

    D. $x + 25 = 25x$

13. If $4x - (3 - x) = 7(x - 3) + 10$, then
    (Rigorous) (Skill 10.1, 10,2)

    A. $x = 8$

    B. $x = -8$

    C. $x = 4$

    D. $x = -4$

14. The price of gas was $3.27 per gallon. Your tank holds 15 gallons of fuel. You are using two tanks a week. How much will you save weekly if the price of gas goes down to $2.30 per gallon.
    (Rigorous) (Skill 11.1, 11.2, 11.3)

    A. $26.00

    B. $29.00

    C. $15.00

    D. $17.00

15. What unit of measurement would describe the spread of a forest fire in a unit time?
    (Easy) (Skill 9.3)

    A. 10 square yards per second

    B. 10 yards per minute

    C. 10 feet per hour

    D. 10 cubit feet per hour

16. In a sample of 40 full-time employees at a particular company, 35 were also holding down a part-time job requiring at least 10 hours/week. If this proportion holds for the entire company of 25000 employees, how many full-time employees at this company are actually holding down a part-time job of at least 10 hours per week.
    (Rigorous) (Skill 12.3)

    A. 714

    B. 625

    C. 21,875

    D. 28,571

17. A student organization is interested in determining how strong the support is among registered voters in the United States for the president's education plan. Which of the following procedures would be most appropriate for selecting a statistically unbiased sample?
(Rigorous) (Skill 4.1, 4.2)

A. Having viewers call in to a nationally broadcast talk show and give their opinions.

B. Survey registered voters selected by blind drawing in the three largest states.

C. Select regions of the country by blind drawing and then select people from the voters registration list by blind drawing.

D. Pass out survey forms at the front entrance of schools selected by blind drawing and ask people entering and exiting to fill them in.

18. The following chart shows the yearly average number of international tourists visiting Palm Beach for 1990-1994. How many more international tourists visited Palm Beach in 1994 than in 1991?
(Easy) (Skill 4.1, 4.2)

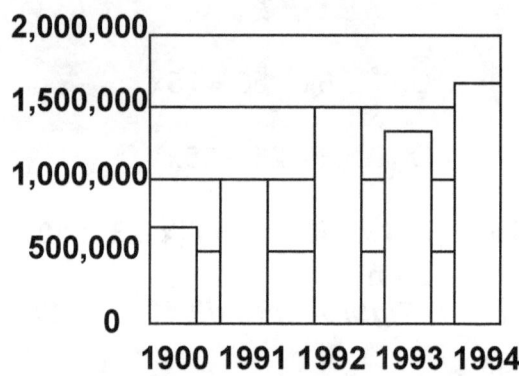

A. 100,000

B. 600,000

C. 1,600,000

D. 8,000,000

19. Consider the graph of the distribution of the length of time it took individuals to complete an employment form.

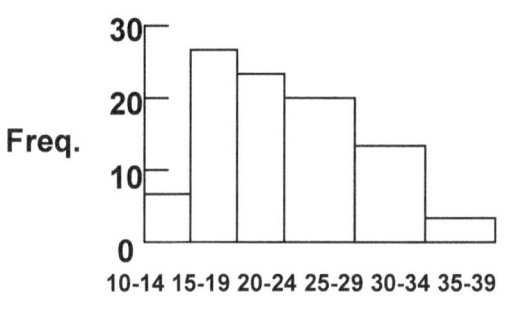

Minutes

Approximately how many individuals took less than 15 minutes to complete the employment form?
(Easy) (Skill 4.1, 4.2)

   A. 35
   B. 28
   C. 7
   D. 4

20. A sofa sells for $520. If the retailer makes a 30% profit, what was the wholesale price?
(Average Rigor) (Skill 12.3)

   A. $400
   B. $676
   C. $490
   D. $364

21. Which statement is true about George's budget?
(Easy) (Skill 4.1, 4.2)

   A. George spends the greatest portion of his income on food.

   B. George spends twice as much on utilities as he does on his mortgage.

   C. George spends twice as much on utilities as he does on food.

   D. George spends the same amount on food and utilities as he does on mortgage.

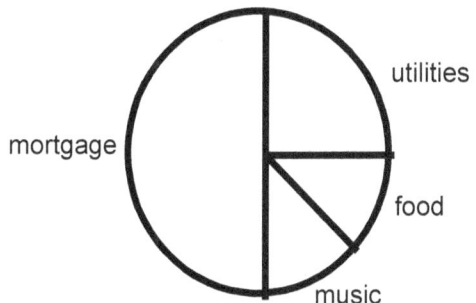

22. 3 km is equivalent to
(Average Rigor) (Skill 9.3)

   A. 300 cm

   B. 300 m

   C. 3000 cm

   D. 3000 m

23. The mass of a cookie is closest to:
    (Average Rigor) (Skill 0/3)

    A. 0.5 kg

    B. 0.5 grams

    C. 15 grams

    D. 1.5 grams

24. 576 + 29 − 57 =
    (Easy) (Skill 10.1, 10.2)

    A. 548

    B. 547

    C. 549

    D. 546

25. 1250 ÷ 50 =
    (Average Rigor) (Skill 11/2)

    A. 20

    B. 25

    C. 15

    D.   40

TEACHER CERTIFICATION STUDY GUIDE

DIRECTIONS : *The passage below contains many errors. Read the passage. Then answer each test item by choosing the option that corrects an error in the underlined portion(s). No more than one underlined error will appear in each item. If no error exists, choose "No change is necessary."*

Climbing to the top of Mount Everest is an adventure. One which everyone--whether physically fit or not--seems eager to try. The trail stretches for miles, the cold temperatures are usually frigid and brutal.

Climbers must endure severel barriers on the way, including other hikers, steep jagged rocks, and lots of snow. Plus, climbers often find the most grueling part of the trip is their climb back down, just when they are feeling greatly exhausted. Climbers who take precautions are likely to find the ascent less arduous than the unprepared. By donning heavy flannel shirts, gloves, and hats, climbers prevented hypothermia, as well as simple frostbite. A pair of rugged boots is also one of the necesities. If climbers are to avoid becoming dehydrated, there is beverages available for them to transport as well.

Once climbers are completely ready to begin their lengthy journey, they can comfortable enjoy the wonderful scenery. Wide rock formations dazzle the observers eyes with shades of gray and white, while the peak forms a triangle that seems to touch the sky. Each of the climbers are reminded of the splendor and magnifisence of Gods great Earth.

26. **Climbing to the top of Mount Everest is an adventure. One which everyone —whether physically fit or not— seems eager to try.**
(Average Rigor) (Skill 7.1)

A. adventure, one
B. people, whether
C. seem
D. No change is necessary

27. **The trail stretches for miles, the cold temperatures are usually frigid and brutal.**
(Average Rigor) (Skill 7.2)

A. trails
B. miles;
C. usual
D. No change is necessary

28. **Climbers must endure severel barriers on the way, including other hikers, steep jagged rocks, and lots of snow.**
(Easy) (Skill 8.3)

A. several
B. on the way: including
C. hikers'
D. No change is necessary

29. **Plus, climbers often find the most grueling part of the trip is their climb back down, just when they are feeling greatly exhausted.**
(Rigorous) (Skill 5.3)

A. his
B. down; just
C. were
D. No change is necessary

30. **Climbers who take precautions are likely to find the ascent less difficult than the unprepared.**
    (Rigorous) (Skill 6.3, 7.3)

    A. Climbers, who
    B. least difficult
    C. then
    D. No change is necessary

31. **A pair of rugged boots is also one of the necesities.**
    (Easy) (Skill 8.3)

    A. are
    B. also, one
    C. necessities
    D. No change is necessary

32. **Once climbers are completely prepared for their lengthy journey, they can comfortable enjoy the wonderful scenery.**
    (Easy) (Skill 6.3)

    A. they're
    B. journey; they
    C. comfortably
    D. No change is necessary

33. **Each of the climbers are reminded of the splendor and magnifisence of God's great Earth.**
    (Rigorous) (Skill 6.1)

    A. is
    B. magnifisence
    C. Gods
    D. No change is necessary

DIRECTIONS: *The passage below contains several errors. Read the passage. Then answer each test item by choosing the option that corrects an error in the underlined portion(s). No more than one underlined error will appear in each item. If no error exists, choose "No change is necessary."*

Every job places different kinds of demands on their employees. For example, whereas such jobs as accounting and bookkeeping require mathematical ability; graphic design requires creative/artistic ability.

Doing good at one job does not usually guarantee success at another. However, one of the elements crucial to all jobs are especially notable: the chance to accomplish a goal.

The accomplishment of the employees varies according to the job. In many jobs the employees become accustom to the accomplishment provided by the work they do every day.

In medicine, for example, every doctor tests him self by treating badly injured or critically ill people. In the operating room, a team of Surgeons, is responsible for operating on many of these patients. In addition to the feeling of accomplishment that the workers achieve, some jobs also give a sense of identity to the employees'. Profesions like law, education, and sales offer huge financial and emotional rewards. Politicians are public servants: who work for the federal and state governments. President bush is basically employed by the American people to make laws and run the country.

Finally; the contributions that employees make to their companies and to the world cannot be taken for granted. Through their work, employees are performing a service for their employers and are contributing something to the world.

34. **Every job <u>places</u> different kinds of demands on <u>their</u> <u>employees</u>.**
    (Rigorous) (Skill 6.1)

    A. place
    B. its
    C. employes
    D. No change is necessary

35. **<u>For example, whereas</u> such jobs as accounting and bookkeeping require mathematical <u>ability;</u> graphic design requires creative/artistic ability.**
    (Rigorous) (Skill 7.3)

    A. For example
    B. whereas,
    C. ability,
    D. No change is necessary

36. **Doing <u>good</u> at one job does not <u>usually</u> guarantee <u>success</u> at another.**
    (Average Rigor) (Skill 6.3)

    A. well
    B. usualy
    C. succeeding
    D. No change is necessary

37. **<u>However,</u> one of the elements crucial to all jobs <u>are</u> especially <u>notable:</u> the accomplishment of a goal.**
    (Rigorous) (Skill 5.1)

    A. However
    B. is
    C. notable;
    D. No change is necessary

38. **The <u>accomplishment</u> of the <u>employees</u> <u>vary</u> according to the job.**
    (Rigorous) (Skill 5.1)

    A. accomplishment,
    B. employee's
    C. varies
    D. No change is necessary

39. **In many jobs the employees <u>become</u> <u>accustom</u> to the accomplishment <u>provided</u> by the work they do every day.**
    (Average Rigor) (Skill 5.2)

    A. became
    B. accustomed
    C. provides
    D. No change is necessary

40. **In medicine, for example, every doctor <u>tests</u> <u>him self</u> by treating badly injured and critically ill people.**
    (Easy) (Skill 6.2)

    A. test
    B. himself
    C. critical
    D. No change is necessary

41. In the <u>operating room,</u> a team of <u>Surgeons, is</u> responsible for operating on many of <u>these</u> patients.
(Average Rigor) (Skill 7.3, 8.2)

   A. operating room:
   B. surgeons is
   C. those
   D. No change is necessary

42. In addition to the feeling of accomplishment that the workers <u>achieve</u>, some jobs also <u>give</u> a sense of self-identity to the <u>employees'</u>.
(Easy) (Skill 6.2)

   A. acheive
   B. gave
   C. employees
   D. No change is necessary

43. <u>Profesions</u> like law, <u>education,</u> and sales <u>offer</u> huge financial and emotional rewards.
(Easy) (Skill 8.3)

   A. Professions
   B. education;
   C. offered
   D. No change is necessary

44. Politicians <u>are</u> public <u>servants: who work</u> for the federal and state governments.
(Average Rigor) (Skill 7.3)

   A. were
   B. servants who
   C. worked
   D. No change is necessary

45. President bush is basically employed <u>by</u> the American people to <u>make</u> laws and run the country.
(Easy) (Skill 8.2)

   A. Bush
   B. to
   C. made
   D. No change is necessary

46. <u>Finally;</u> the contributions that employees make to <u>their</u> companies and to the world cannot be <u>taken</u> for granted.
(Average Rigor) (Skill 7.3)

   A. Finally,
   B. their
   C. took
   D. No change is necessary

DIRECTIONS: *For the underlined sentence(s), choose the option that expresses the meaning with the most fluency and the clearest logic within the context. If the underlined sentence should not be changed, choose Option A, which shows no change.*

47. Selecting members of a President's cabinet can often be an aggravating process. <u>Either there are too many or too few qualified candidates for a certain position, and then they have to be confirmed by the Senate, where there is the possibility of rejection.</u>
(Rigorous) (Skill 2.3 2.4, 14.1)

   A. Either there are too many or too few qualified candidate for a certain position, and then they have to be confirmed by the Senate, where there is the possibility of rejection.

   B. Qualified candidates for certain positions face the possibility of rejection, when they have to be confirmed by the Senate.

   C. The Senate has to confirm qualified candidates, who face the possibility of rejection.

   D. Because the Senate has to confirm qualified candidates; they face the possibility of rejection.

48. Treating patients for drug and/or alcohol abuse is a sometimes difficult process. <u>Even though there are a number of different methods for helping the patient overcome a dependency, there is no way of knowing which is best in the long-run.</u>
(Rigorous) (Skill 2.3, 2.4, 14.1)

   A. Even though there are a number of different methods for helping the patient overcome a dependency, there is no way of knowing which is best in the long-run.

   B. Even though different methods can help a patient overcome a dependency, there is no way to know which is best in the long-run.

   C. Even though there is no way to know which way is best in the long run, patients can overcome their dependencies when they are helped.

   D. There is no way to know which method will help the patient overcome a dependency in the long-run, even though there are many different ones.

49. **Many factors account for the decline in quality of public education. Overcrowding, budget cutbacks, and societal deterioration which have greatly affected student learning.**
(Average Rigor) (Skill 2.3, 2.4, 14.1)

A. Overcrowding, budget cutbacks, and societal deterioration which have greatly affected student learning.

B. Student learning has been greatly affected by overcrowding, budget cutbacks, and societal deterioration.

C. Due to overcrowding, budget cutbacks, and societal deterioration, student learning has been greatly affected.

D. Overcrowding, budget cutbacks, and societal deterioration have affected students learning greatly.

DIRECTIONS: *Choose the sentence that logically and correctly expresses the comparison.*
(Average Rigor) (Skill 6.3)

50. A. The Empire State Building in New York is taller than buildings in the city.

B. The Empire State Building in New York is taller than any other building in the city.

C. The Empire State Building in New York is tallest than other buildings in the city.

DIRECTIONS: *Choose the most ineffective word within the context of the sentence.*

51. **Considered by many to be one of the worst terrorist incidents on American soil was the bombing of the Oklahoma City Federal Building which will be remembered for years to come.**
(Average Rigor) (Skill 1.1)

A. considered by many to be
B. terrorist
C. on American soil
D. for years to come

ATAS

52. The <u>flu</u> epidemic struck <u>most of</u> the <u>respected</u> faculty and students of The Woolbright School, forcing the Boynton Beach School Superintendent to close it down <u>for two weeks</u>.
    (Average Rigor) (Skill 1.1)

    A. flu
    B. most of
    C. respected
    D. for two weeks

53. The <u>expanding</u> number of television channels has <u>prompted</u> cable operators to raise their prices, <u>even though</u> many consumers do not want to pay a higher <u>increased</u> amount for their service.
    (Average Rigor) (Skill 1.1)

    A. expanding
    B. prompted
    C. even though
    D. increased

DIRECTIONS: Read the following paragraph and answer the questions that follow.

This writer has often been asked to tutor hospitalized children with cystic fibrosis. While undergoing all the precautionary measures to see these children (i.e. scrubbing thoroughly and donning sterilized protective gear- for the child's protection), she has often wondered why their parents subject these children to the pressures of schooling and trying to catch up on what they have missed because of hospitalization, which is a normal part of cystic fibrosis patients' lives. These children undergo so many tortuous treatments a day that it seems cruel to expect them to learn as normal children do, especially with their life expectancies being as short as they are.

54. What is meant by the word "precautionary" in the second sentence?
    (Average Rigor) (Skill 1.1)

    A. Careful
    B. Protective
    C. Medical
    D. Sterilizing

55. What is the main idea of this passage?
    (Rigorous) (Skill 2.4)

    A. There is a lot of preparation involved in visiting a patient of cystic fibrosis.
    B. Children with cystic fibrosis are incapable of living normal lives.
    C. Certain concessions should be made for children with cystic fibrosis.
    D. Children with cystic fibrosis die young.

56. What is the author's tone?
    (Rigorous) (Skill 13.3)

    A. Sympathetic
    B. Cruel
    C. Disbelieving
    D. Cheerful

57. What is the author's purpose?
    (Rigorous) (Skill 13.3)

    A. To inform
    B. To entertain
    C. To describe
    D. To narrate

58. What type of organizational pattern is the author using?
    (Rigorous) (Skill 3.1)

    A. Classification
    B. Explanation
    C. Comparison and contrast
    D. Cause and effect

59. The author states that it is "cruel" to expect children with cystic fibrosis to learn as "normal" children do. Is this a fact or an opinion?
    (Average Rigor) (Skill 4.3)

    A. Fact
    B. Opinion

60. Is there evidence of bias in this paragraph?
    (Average Rigor) (Skill 13.3)

    A. Yes
    B. No

61. What kind of relationship is found within the last sentence which starts with "These children undergo..." and ends with "...as short as they are"?
    (Rigorous) (Skill 3.1)

    A. Addition
    B. Explanation
    C. Generalization
    D. Classification

62. Does the author present an argument that is valid or invalid concerning the schooling of children with cystic fibrosis?
    (Rigorous) (Skill 13.3)

    A. Valid
    B. Invalid

DIRECTIONS: Read the following passage and answer the questions that follow.

Disciplinary practices have been found to affect diverse areas of child development such as the acquisition of moral values, obedience to authority, and performance at school. Even though the dictionary has a specific Definition of the word "discipline," it is still open to interpretation by people of different cultures.

There are four types of disciplinary styles: assertion of power, withdrawal of love, reasoning, and permissiveness. Assertion of power involves the use of force to discourage unwanted behavior. Withdrawal of love involves making the love of a parent conditional on a child's good behavior. Reasoning involves persuading the child to behave one way rather than another. Permissiveness involves allowing the child to do as he or she pleases and face the consequences of his/her actions.

63. What is the meaning of the word "diverse" in the first sentence?
(Easy) (Skill 1.1)

   A. Many
   B. Related to children
   C. Disciplinary
   D. Moral

64. Name the four types of disciplinary styles.
(Easy) (Skill 2.0)

   A. Reasoning, power assertion, morality, and permissiveness.
   B. Morality, reasoning, permissiveness, and withdrawal of love.
   C. Withdrawal of love, permissiveness, assertion of power, and reasoning.
   D. Permissiveness, morality, reasoning, and power assertion.

65. What organizational structure is used in the first sentence of the second paragraph?
(Average Rigor) (Skill 13.3)

   A. Addition
   B. Explanation
   C. Definition
   D. Simple listing

66. What is the main idea of this passage?
(Rigorous) (Skill 2.1)

   A. Different people have different ideas of what discipline is.
   B. Permissiveness is the most widely used disciplinary style.
   C. Most people agree on their definition of discipline.
   D. There are four disciplinary styles.

67. Is this passage biased?
   (Rigorous) (Skill 13.3)

   A. Yes
   B. No

68. What is the author's tone?
   (Rigorous) (Skill 13.3)

   A. Disbelieving
   B. Angry
   C. Informative
   D. Optimistic

69. The author states that "assertion of power involves the use of force to discourage unwanted behavior." Is this a fact or an opinion?
   (Average Rigor) (Skill 4.3)

   A. Fact
   B. Opinion

70. From reading this passage we can conclude that
   (Average Rigor) (Skill 13.3)

   A. The author is a teacher.
   B. The author has many children.
   C. The author has written a book about discipline.
   D. The author has done a lot of research on discipline.

DIRECTIONS: *Read the following passage and answer the questions that follow.*

One of the most difficult problems plaguing American education is the assessment of teachers. No one denies that teachers ought to be answerable for what they do, but what exactly does that mean? The Oxford American Dictionary defines accountability as: the obligation to give a reckoning or explanation for one's actions.

Does a student have to learn for teaching to have taken place? Historically, teaching has not been defined in this restrictive manner; the teacher was thought to be responsible for the quantity and quality of material covered and the way in which it was presented. However, some definitions of teaching now imply that students must learn in order for teaching to have taken place.

As a teacher who tries my best to keep current on all the latest teaching strategies, I believe that those teachers who do not bother even to pick up an educational journal every once in a while should be kept under close watch. There are many teachers out there who have been teaching for decades and refuse to change their ways even if research has proven that their methods are outdated and ineffective. There is no place in the profession of teaching for these types of individuals. It is time that the American educational system clean house, for the sake of our children.

71. **What is the meaning of the word "reckoning" in the third sentence?**
(Easy) (Skill 1.1)

A. Thought
B. Answer
C. Obligation
D. Explanation

72. **What is the main idea of the passage?**
(Rigorous) (Skill 2.1)

A. Teachers should not be answerable for what they do.
B. Teachers who do not do their job should be fired.
C. The author is a good teacher.
D. Assessment of teachers is a serious problem in society today.

73. **From the passage, one can infer that**
(Rigorous) (Skill 13.3)

A. The author considers herself a good teacher.
B. Poor teachers will be fired.
C. Students have to learn for teaching to take place.
D. The author will be fired.

74. Teachers who do not keep current on educational trends should be fired. Is this a fact or an opinion?
    (Average Rigor) (Skill 4.3)

    A. Fact
    B. Opinion

75. The author states that teacher assessment is a problem for
    (Average Rigor) (Skill 13.3)

    A. Elementary schools
    B. Secondary schools
    C. American education
    D. Families

76. What is the author's purpose in writing this?
    (Average Rigor) (Skill 13.3)

    A. To entertain
    B. To narrate
    C. To describe
    D. To persuade

77. Is there evidence of bias in this passage?
    (Rigorous) (Skill 13.3)

    A. Yes
    B. No

78. What is the author's overall organizational pattern?
    (Rigorous) (Skill 13.3)

    A. Classification
    B. Cause and effect
    C. Definition
    D. Comparison and contrast

79. The author's tone is one of
    (Rigorous) (Skill 13.3)

    A. Disbelief
    B. Excitement
    C. Support
    D. Concern

80. What is meant by the word "plaguing" in the first sentence?
    (Average Rigor) (Skill 1.1)

    A. Causing problems
    B. Causing illness
    C. Causing anger
    D. Causing failure

81. Where does the author get her definition of "accountability?"
    (Average Rigor) (Skill 1.1)

    A. Webster's Dictionary
    B. Encyclopedia Brittanica
    C. Oxford Dictionary
    D. World Book Encyclopedia

82. What development patterns should a professional teacher assess to meet the needs of the students?
    (Rigorous) (Skill 13.1)

    A. Academic, regional and family background
    B. Social, physical, academic
    C. Academic, physical and family background
    D. Physical, family and ethnic background

83. The use of technology in the classroom allows for
    (Average Rigor) (Skill 13.2)

    A. More complex lessons
    B. Better delivery of instruction
    C. Variety of instruction
    D. Better ability to meet more individual student needs

84. To promote word study, children can
    (Average Rigor) (Skill 13.2)

    A. Be required to go to the dictionary at least once or twice a day.
    B. Collect and share words of interest they find in their readings.
    C. Do vocabulary work sheets from a basal reader or commercial vocabulary book.
    D. Do all of the above.

85. How can students use a computer desktop publishing center?
    (Average Rigor) (Skill 13.2)

    A. To set up a classroom budget
    B. To create student made books
    C. To design a research project
    D. To create a classroom behavior management system

86. To help students with "main idea" questions, the teacher should
    (Average Rigor) (Skill 13.3)

    A. Give out a strategy sheet on the main idea for children to place their reader's notebooks.
    B. Model responding to such a question as part of guided reading.
    C. Have children create "main idea questions" to go with their writings
    D. All of the above.

87. Dictionary study
    (Average Rigor) (Skill 13.2)

    A. Can begin in grades 1 or 2.
    B. Can begin in pre-K using the lush picture dictionaries.
    C. Should start on grade three level.
    D. A and b.

88. Children "own" words when all of the following happen except
    (Average Rigor) (Skill 13.2)

    A. They find these words on their own.
    B. The teacher provides a mandated word list.
    C. They use the words in their own writings.
    D. The words appear in literature that interests them.

89. One of the many ways in which a child can demonstrate comprehension of a story is by:
(Average rigor) *(Skill 13.3)*

A. Filling in a strategy sheet.
B. Retelling the story orally.
C. Retelling the story in writing.
D. All of the above.

90. Making inferences from the text means that the reader:
(Rigorous) *(Skill 13.3)*

A. Is making informed judgments based on available evidence.
B. Is making a guess based on prior experiences.
C. Is making a guess based on what the reader would like to be true of the text.
D. All of the above

Answer Key

1.	D	31.	C	61.	B
2.	A	32.	C	62.	B
3.	C	33.	A	63.	A
4.	A	34.	B	64.	C
5.	D	35.	C	65.	D
6.	C	36.	A	66.	A
7.	C	37.	B	67.	B
8.	B	38.	C	68.	C
9.	C	39.	B	69.	A
10.	C	40.	B	70.	D
11.	D	41.	B	71.	D
12.	A	42.	C	72.	D
13.	C	43.	A	73.	A
14.	B	44.	B	74.	B
15.	A	45.	A	75.	C
16.	C	46.	A	76.	D
17.	C	47.	C	77.	A
18.	B	48.	B	78.	C
19.	C	49.	B	79.	D
20.	A	50.	B	80.	A
21.	C	51.	A	81.	C
22.	D	52.	C	82.	B
23.	C	53.	D	83.	D
24.	A	54.	B	84.	D
25.	B	55.	C	85.	B
26.	A	56.	A	86.	D
27.	B	57.	C	87.	D
28.	A	58.	B	88.	B
29.	D	59.	B	89.	D
30.	D	60.	A	90.	A

Rigor Table

	Easy %20	Average Rigor %40	Rigorous %40
Question #	1, 10, 11, 15, 18, 19, 21, 24, 28, 31, 32, 40, 42, 43, 45, 63, 64, 71	3, 4, 20, 22, 23, 25, 26, 27, 36, 39, 41, 44, 46, 49, 50, 51, 52, 53, 54, 59, 60, 65, 69, 70, 74, 75, 76, 80, 82, 83, 84, 85, 86, 87, 88, 89	2,5,6,7,8,9,12, 13, 14,16, 17, 29, 30, 33, 34, 35, 37, 38, 47, 48, 55, 56, 57, 58, 61, 62, 66, 67, 68, 72, 73, 77, 78, 79, 82, 90

TEACHER CERTIFICATION STUDY GUIDE

Rationales for Sample Questions

1. $\left(\dfrac{-4}{9}\right) + \left(\dfrac{-7}{10}\right) =$

   (Easy) (Skill 12.2)

   A. $\dfrac{23}{90}$

   B. $\dfrac{-23}{90}$

   C. $\dfrac{103}{90}$

   D. $\dfrac{-103}{90}$

   Answer: D -- $\dfrac{-103}{90}$

   Rationale: Find the LCD of $\dfrac{-4}{9}$ and $\dfrac{-7}{10}$. The LCD is 90, so you get $\dfrac{-40}{90} + \dfrac{-63}{90} = \dfrac{-103}{90}$.

2. $(5.6) \times (-0.11) =$

   (Rigorous) (Skill 12.2)

   A. -0.616
   B. 0.616
   C. -6.110
   D. 6.110

   Answer: A -- -0.616

   Rationale: Simple multiplication. The answer will be negative because a positive times a negative is a negative number. $5.6 \times -0.11 = -0.616$

ASSESS. OF TEACH. ASSIST. SKILLS

3. $4\frac{2}{9} \times \frac{7}{10}$
   (Average Rigor) (Skill 12.1)

   A. $4\frac{9}{10}$
   B. $\frac{266}{90}$
   C. $2\frac{43}{45}$
   D. $2\frac{6}{20}$

   Answer: C -- $2\frac{43}{45}$

   Rationale: Convert any mixed number to an improper fraction: $\frac{38}{9} \times \frac{7}{10}$. Since no common factors of numerators or denominators exist, multiply the numerators and the denominators by each other = $\frac{266}{90}$. Convert back to a mixed number and reduce $2\frac{86}{90} = 2\frac{43}{45}$.

4. 0.74 =
   (Average Rigor) (Skill 12.2, 12.4)

   A. $\frac{74}{100}$
   B. 7.4%
   C. $\frac{33}{50}$
   D. $\frac{74}{10}$

   Answer: A – $\frac{74}{100}$

   Rationale: 0.74→the 4 is in the hundredths place, so the answer is $\frac{74}{100}$

5. **303 is what percent of 600?**
   (Rigorous) (Skill 12.3)

   A. 0.505%
   B. 5.05%
   C. 505%
   D. 50.5%

   Answer: D – 50.5%.

   Rationale: 5. Use x for the percent. $600x = 303$.
   $\dfrac{600x}{600} = \dfrac{303}{600} \to x = 0.505 = 50.5\%$,

6. **An item that sells for $375 is put on sale at $120. What is the percent of decrease?**
   (Rigorous) (Skill 12.3)

   A. 25%
   B. 28%
   C. 68%
   D. 34%

   Answer: C – 68%

   Rationale: Use $(1 - x)$ as the discount. $375x = 120$.
   $375(1-x) = 120 \to 375 - 375x = 120 \to 375x = 255 \to x = 0.68 = 68\%$

7. **Two mathematics classes have a total of 410 students. The 8:00 am class has 40 more than the 10:00 am class. How many students are in the 10:00 am class?**
   (Rigorous) (Skill 12.3)

   A. 123.3
   B. 370
   C. 185
   D. 330

   Answer: C -- 185

   Rationale: Let x = # of students in the 8 am class and $x - 40$ = # of students in the 10 am class.
   $x + (x - 40) = 410 \to 2x - 40 = 410 \to 2x = 450 \to x = 225$. So there are 225 students in the 8 am class, and $225 - 40 = 185$ in the 10 am class.

8. A restaurant employs 465 people. There are 280 waiters and 185 cooks. If 168 waiters and 85 cooks receive pay raises, what percent of the waiters will receive a pay raise?
   (Rigorous) (Skill 12.3)

   A. 36.13%
   B. 60%
   C. 60.22%
   D. 40%

   Answer: B – 60%

   Rationale: The total number of waiters is 280 and only 168 of them get a pay raise. Divide the number getting a raise by the total number of waiters to get the percent. $\frac{168}{280} = 0.6 = 60\%$.

9. Round $1\frac{13}{16}$ of an inch to the nearest quarter of an inch.
   (Rigorous) (Skill 12.1, 12.4)

   A. $1\frac{1}{4}$ inch
   B. $1\frac{5}{8}$ inch
   C. $1\frac{3}{4}$ inch
   D. 2 inches

   Answer: C – $1\frac{3}{4}$ inch

   Rationale: $01\frac{13}{16}$ inches is approximately $1\frac{12}{16}$, which is also $1\frac{3}{4}$, which is the nearest $\frac{1}{4}$ of an inch.

10. **What unit of measurement could we use to report the distance traveled walking around a track?**
    (Easy) (Skill 9.3)

    A. degrees
    B. square meters
    C. kilometers
    D. cubic feet

    Answer: C – kilometers

    Rationale: Degrees measures angles, square meters measures area, cubic feet measure volume, and kilometers measures length. Kilometers is the only reasonable answer.

11. $\frac{7}{9} + \frac{1}{3} \div \frac{2}{3} =$
    (Easy) (Skill 12.1)

    A. $\frac{5}{3}$
    B. $\frac{3}{2}$
    C. 2
    D. $\frac{23}{18}$

    Answer: D – $\frac{23}{18}$

    Rationale: First, do the division. $\frac{1}{3} \div \frac{2}{3} = \frac{1}{3} \times \frac{3}{2} = \frac{1}{2}$ Add. $\frac{7}{9} + \frac{1}{2} = \frac{14}{18} + \frac{9}{18} = \frac{23}{18}$

TEACHER CERTIFICATION STUDY GUIDE

12. Choose the equation that is equivalent to the following:
$\frac{3x}{5} - 5 = 5x$

(Rigorous) (Skill 12.4)

A. $3x - 25 = 25x$
B. $x - \frac{25}{3} = 25x$
C. $6x - 50 = 75x$
D. $x + 25 = 25x$

Answer: A –

Rationale: A is the correct answer because it is the original equation multiplied by 5. The other choices alter the answer to the original equation.

13. If $4x - (3 - x) = 7(x - 3) + 10$, then
(Rigorous) (Skill 10.1, 10,2)

A. x = 8
B. x = -8
C. x = 4
D. x = -4

Answer: C – x = 4

Rationale: Solve for x.

$$4x - (3 - x) = 7(x - 3) + 10$$
$$4x - 3 + x = 7x - 21 + 10$$
$$5x - 3 = 7x - 11$$
$$5x = 7x - 11 + 3$$
$$5x - 7x = ^-8$$
$$^-2x = ^-8$$
$$x = 4$$

14. The price of gas was $3.27 per gallon. Your tank holds 15 gallons of fuel. You are using two tanks a week. How much will you save weekly if the price of gas goes down to $2.30 per gallon.
    (Rigorous) (Skill 11.1, 11.2, 11.3)

    A. $26.00
    B. $29.00
    C. $15.00
    D. $17.00

    Answer: B -- $29.00

    Rationale: 15 gallons x 2 tanks = 30 gallons a week
    = 30 gallons x $3.27 = $98.10
    30 gallons x $2.30 = $69.00
    $98.10 - $69.00 = $29.10 is approximately $29.00.

15. What unit of measurement would describe the spread of a forest fire in a unit time?
    (Easy) (Skill 9.3)

    A. 10 square yards per second
    B. 10 yards per minute
    C. 10 feet per hour
    D. 10 cubit feet per hour

    Answer: A – 10 square yards per second

    Rationale: The only appropriate answer is one that describes "an area" of forest consumed per unit time. All answers are not units of area measurement except answer **A**.

TEACHER CERTIFICATION STUDY GUIDE

16. In a sample of 40 full-time employees at a particular company, 35 were also holding down a part-time job requiring at least 10 hours/week. If this proportion holds for the entire company of 25000 employees, how many full-time employees at this company are actually holding down a part-time job of at least 10 hours per week. *(Rigorous) (Skill 12.3)*

   A. 714
   B. 625
   C. 21,875
   D. 28,571

   Answer: C – 21,875

   Rationale: $\frac{35}{40}$ full time employees have a part time job also. Out of 25,000 full time employees, the number that also have a part time job is $\frac{35}{40} = \frac{x}{25000} \rightarrow 40x = 875000 \rightarrow x = 21875$, so 21875 full time employees also have a part time job.

17. A student organization is interested in determining how strong the support is among registered voters in the United States for the president's education plan. Which of the following procedures would be most appropriate for selecting a statistically unbiased sample? *(Rigorous) (Skill 4.1, 4.2)*

   A. Having viewers call in to a nationally broad-cast talk show and give their opinions.
   B. Survey registered voters selected by blind drawing in the three largest states.
   C. Select regions of the country by blind drawing and then select people from the voters registration list by blind drawing.
   D. Pass out survey forms at the front entrance of schools selected by blind drawing and ask people entering and exiting to fill them in.

   Answer: C – Select regions of the country by blind drawing and then select people from the voters registration list by blind drawing.

   Rationale: is the best answer because it is random and it surveys a larger population.

18. The following chart shows the yearly average number of international tourists visiting Palm Beach for 1990-1994. How many more international tourists visited Palm Beach in 1994 than in 1991? *(Easy) (Skill 4.1, 4.2)*

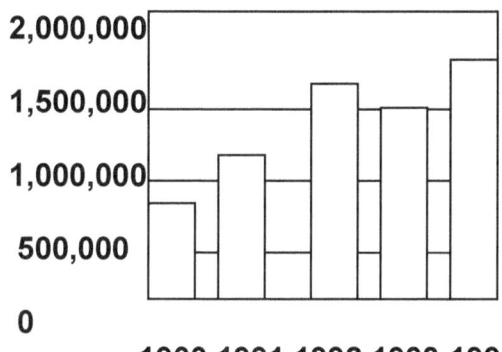

A. 100,000
B. 600,000
C. 1,600,000
D. 8,000,000

Answer: B – 600,000

Rationale: The number of tourists in 1991 was 1,000,000 and the number in 1994 was 1,600,000. Subtract to get a difference of 600,000, which is answer **B**.

19. Consider the graph of the distribution of the length of time it took individuals to complete an employment form.

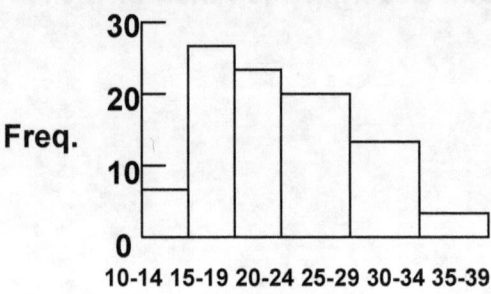

Approximately how many individuals took less than 15 minutes to complete the employment form? *(Easy) (Skill 4.1, 4.2)*

    A.   35
    B.   28
    C.   7
    D.   4

Answer: C – 7

Rationale: According to the chart, the number of people who took under 15 minutes is 7.

20. A sofa sells for $520. If the retailer makes a 30% profit, what was the wholesale price?
(Average Rigor) (Skill 12.3)

    A. $400
    B. $676
    C. $490
    D. $364

Answer: A -- $400

Rationale: $400; Let x be the wholesale price, then $x + .30x = 520$, $1.30x = 520$, divide both sides by 1.30.

21. **Which statement is true about George's budget?**
    (Easy) (Skill 4.1, 4.2)

    A. George spends the greatest portion of his income on food.
    B. George spends twice as much on utilities as he does on his mortgage.
    C. George spends twice as much on utilities as he does on food.
    D. George spends the same amount on food and utilities as he does on mortgage.

    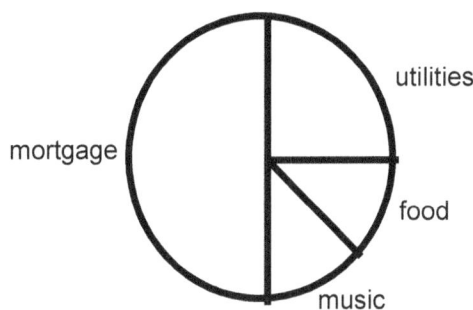

    Answer: C – George spends twice as much on utilities as he does on food.

    Rationale: George spends twice as much on utilities as on food, so the answer is C.

22. **3 km is equivalent to** *(Average Rigor) (Skill 9.3)*

    A. 300 cm
    B. 300 m
    C. 3000 cm
    D. 3000 m

    Answer: D – 3000 m

    Rationale: To change kilometers to meters, move the decimal 3 places to the right.

23. The mass of a cookie is closest to: *(Average Rigor) (Skill 0/3)*

    A. 0.5 kg
    B. 0.5 grams
    C. 15 grams
    D. 1.5 grams

    Answer: C – 15 grams

    Rationale:

24. 576 + 29 – 57 =
    (Easy) (Skill 10.1, 10.2)

    A. 548
    B. 547
    C. 549
    D. 546

    Answer: A – 548

    Rationale:
    ```
      1 1
      576
    +  29
      605
    ```

    ```
     5 9 15
      605
    -  57
      548
    ```

TEACHER CERTIFICATION STUDY GUIDE

25. $1250 \div 50 =$
    (Average Rigor) (Skill 11/2)

    A. 20
    B. 25
    C. 15
    D. 40

    Answer: B – 25

    Rationale:

    $$50 \overline{)1250}$$

    $$\begin{array}{r} 2 \\ 50 \overline{)1250} \end{array}$$

    $$\begin{array}{r} 2 \\ 50 \overline{)1250} \\ -100 \\ \hline 250 \end{array}$$

    $$\begin{array}{r} 25 \\ 50 \overline{)1250} \\ -100 \\ \hline 250 \\ -250 \\ \hline 0 \end{array}$$

DIRECTIONS: *The passage below contains many errors. Read the passage. Then answer each test item by choosing the option that corrects an error in the underlined portion(s). No more than one underlined error will appear in each item. If no error exists, choose "No change is necessary."*

    Climbing to the top of Mount Everest is an adventure. One which everyone--whether physically fit or not--seems eager to try. The trail stretches for miles, the cold temperatures are usually frigid and brutal.
    Climbers must endure several barriers on the way, including other hikers, steep jagged rocks, and lots of snow. Plus, climbers often find the most grueling part of the trip is their climb back down, just when they are feeling greatly exhausted. Climbers who take precautions are likely to find the ascent less arduous than the unprepared. By donning heavy flannel shirts, gloves, and hats, climbers prevented hypothermia, as well as simple frostbite. A pair of rugged boots is also one of the necessities. If climbers are to avoid becoming dehydrated, there is beverages available for them to transport as well.
    Once climbers are completely ready to begin their lengthy journey, they can comfortable enjoy the wonderful scenery. Wide rock formations dazzle the observers eyes with shades of gray and white, while the peak forms a triangle that seems to touch the sky. Each of the climbers are reminded of the splendor and magnificence of Gods great Earth.

26. **Climbing to the top of Mount Everest is an <u>adventure. One</u> which everyone —<u>whether</u> physically fit or not— <u>seems</u> eager to try. *(Average Rigor) (Skill 7.1)***

    A.   adventure, one
    B.   people, whether
    C.   seem
    D.   No change is necessary

Answer: A – adventure, one

Rationale: A comma is needed between *adventure* and *one* to avoid creating a fragment of the second part. In Option B, a comma after *everyone* would not be appropriate when the dash is used on the other side of *not*. In Option C, the singular verb *seems* is needed to agree with the singular subject *everyone*.

27. The trail stretches for miles, the cold temperatures are usually frigid and brutal. *(Average Rigor) (Skill 7.2)*

   A. trails
   B. miles;
   C. usual
   D. No change is necessary

   Answer: B – miles;

   Rationale: A semicolon, not a comma, is needed to separate the first independent clause from the second independent clause. Option A is incorrect because the plural subject *trails* needs the singular verb stretch. Option C is incorrect because the adverb form *usually* is needed to modify the adjective *frigid*.

28. Climbers must endure severel barriers on the way, including other hikers, steep jagged rocks, and lots of snow.
   (Easy) (Skill 8.3)

   A. several
   B. on the way: including
   C. hikers
   D. No change is necessary

   Answer: A – several

   Rationale: The word *several* is misspelled in the text. Option B is incorrect because a comma, not a colon, is needed to set off the modifying phrase. Option C is incorrect because no apostrophe is needed after *hikers* since possession is not involved.

29.

29. Plus, climbers often find the most grueling part of the trip is <u>their</u> climb back <u>down, just</u> when they <u>are</u> feeling greatly exhausted.
(Rigorous) (Skill 5.3)

   A. his
   B. down; just
   C. were
   D. No change is necessary

   Answer: D – No change is necessary

   Rationale: The present tense must be used consistently throughout, therefore Option C is incorrect. Option A is incorrect because the singular pronoun *his* does not agree with the plural antecedent *climbers*. Option B is incorrect because a comma, not a semicolon, is needed to separate the dependent clause from the main clause.

30. Climbers <u>who</u> take precautions are likely to find the ascent <u>less difficult</u> <u>than</u> the unprepared.
(Rigorous) (Skill 6.3, 7.3)

   A. Climbers, who
   B. least difficult
   C. then
   D. No change is necessary

   Answer: D – No change is necessary

   Rationale: No change is needed. Option A is incorrect because a comma would make the phrase *who take precautions* seem less restrictive or less essential to the sentence. Option B is incorrect because *less* is appropriate when two items--the prepared and the unprepared--are compared. Option C is incorrect because the comparative adverb *than*, not *then*, is needed.

31. A pair of rugged boots is also one of the necesities. *(Easy) (Skill 8.3)*

   A. are
   B. also, one
   C. necessities
   D. No change is necessary

   Answer: C – necessities

   Rationale: The word *necessities* is misspelled in the text. Option A is incorrect because the singular verb *is* must agree with the singular noun *pair* (a collective singular). Option B is incorrect because *if also* is set off with commas (potential correction), it should be set off on both sides.

32. Once climbers are completely prepared for their lengthy journey, they can comfortable enjoy the wonderful scenery. *(Easy) (Skill 6.3)*

   A. they're
   B. journey; they
   C. comfortably
   D. No change is necessary

   Answer: C – comfortably

   Rationale: The adverb form *comfortably* is needed to modify the verb phrase *can enjoy*. Option A is incorrect because the possessive plural pronoun is spelled *their*. Option B is incorrect because a semi-colon would make the first half of the item seem like an independent clause when the subordinating conjunction *once* makes that clause dependent.

33. Each of the climbers are reminded of the splendor and magnificence of God's great Earth. *(Rigorous) (Skill 6.1)*

   A. is
   B. magnifisence
   C. Gods
   D. No change is necessary

   Answer: A – is

   Rationale: The singular verb *is* agrees with the singular subject *each*. Option B is incorrect because *magnificence* is misspelled. Option C is incorrect because an apostrophe is needed to show possession.

TEACHER CERTIFICATION STUDY GUIDE

DIRECTIONS: *The passage below contains several errors. Read the passage. Then answer each test item by choosing the option that corrects an error in the underlined portion(s). No more than one underlined error will appear in each item. If no error exists, choose "No change is necessary."*

      Every job places different kinds of demands on their employees. For example, whereas such jobs as accounting and bookkeeping require mathematical ability; graphic design requires creative/artistic ability. Doing good at one job does not usually guarantee success at another. However, one of the elements crucial to all jobs are especially notable: the chance to accomplish a goal.

      The accomplishment of the employees varies according to the job. In many jobs the employees become accustom to the accomplishment provided by the work they do every day.

      In medicine, for example, every doctor tests him self by treating badly injured or critically ill people. In the operating room, a team of Surgeons is responsible for operating on many of these patients. In addition to the feeling of accomplishment that the workers achieve, some jobs also give a sense of identity to the employees'. Profesions like law, education, and sales offer huge financial and emotional rewards. Politicians are public servants: who work for the federal and state governments. President bush is basically employed by the American people to make laws and run the country.

      Finally; the contributions that employees make to their companies and to the world cannot be taken for granted. Through their work, employees are performing a service for their employers and are contributing something to the world.

34. Every job <u>places</u> different kinds of demands on <u>their employees</u>. *(Rigorous) (Skill 6.1)*

    A. place
    B. its
    C. employees
    D. No change is necessary

Answer: B – its

Rationale: The singular possessive pronoun *its* must agree with its antecedent *job*, which is singular also. Option A is incorrect because *place* is a plural form and the subject, *job*, is singular. Option C is incorrect because the correct spelling of employees is given in the sentence.

TEACHER CERTIFICATION STUDY GUIDE

35. <u>For example,</u> <u>whereas</u> such jobs as accounting and bookkeeping require mathematical <u>ability;</u> graphic design requires creative/artistic ability.
    (Rigorous) (Skill 7.3)

    A. For example
    B. whereas,
    C. ability,
    D. No change is necessary

    Answer: C – ability,

    Rationale: An introductory dependent clause is set off with a comma, not a semicolon. Option A is incorrect because the transitional phrase *for example* should be set off with a comma. Option B is incorrect because the adverb *whereas* functions like *while* and does not take a comma after it.

36. Doing <u>good</u> at one job does not <u>usually</u> guarantee <u>success</u> at another. *(Average Rigor) (Skill 6.3)*

    A. well
    B. usualy
    C. succeeding
    D. No change is necessary

    Answer: A -- well

    Rationale: The adverb *well* modifies the word *doing*. Option B is incorrect because *usually* is spelled correctly in the sentence. Option C is incorrect because *succeeding* is in the wrong tense.

37. <u>However,</u> one of the elements crucial to all jobs <u>are</u> especially <u>notable:</u> the accomplishment of a goal. *(Rigorous) (Skill 5.1)*

    A. However
    B. is
    C. notable;
    D. No change is necessary

    Answer: B -- is

    Rationale: The singular verb *is* is needed to agree with the singular subject *one*. Option A is incorrect because a comma is needed to set off the transitional word *however*. Option C is incorrect because a colon, not a semicolon, is needed to set off an item.

TEACHER CERTIFICATION STUDY GUIDE

38. The accomplishment of the <u>employees</u> <u>vary</u> according to the job. *(Rigorous) (Skill 5.1)*

    A. accomplishment,
    B. employee's
    C. varies
    D. No change is necessary

    Answer: C -- varies

    Rationale: The singular verb *varies* is needed to agree with the singular subject *accomplishment*. Option A is incorrect because a comma after *accomplishment* would suggest that the modifying phrase of the employees is additional instead of essential. Option B is incorrect because employees is not possessive.

39. In many jobs the employees <u>become</u> <u>accustom</u> to the accomplishment <u>provided</u> by the work they do every day. *(Average Rigor) (Skill 5.2)*

    A. became
    B. accustomed
    C. provides
    D. No change is necessary

    Answer: B -- accustomed

    Rationale: The past participle *accustomed* is needed with the verb *become*. Option A is incorrect because the verb tense does not need to change to the past *became*. Option C is incorrect because *provides* is the wrong tense.

40. In medicine, for example, every doctor <u>tests</u> <u>him self</u> by treating badly injured and <u>critically</u> ill people.
    (Easy) (Skill 6.2)

    A. test
    B. himself
    C. critical
    D. No change is necessary

    Answer: B -- himself

    Rationale: The reflexive pronoun *himself* is needed. (Him self is nonstandard and never correct.) Option A is incorrect because the singular verb test is needed to agree with the singular subject doctor. Option C is incorrect because the adverb *critically* is needed to modify the verb *ill*.

41. In the operating room, a team of Surgeons, is responsible for operating on many of these patients.
    (Average Rigor) (Skill 7.3, 8.2)

    A. operating room:
    B. surgeons is
    C. those
    D. No change is necessary

    Answer: B – surgeons is

    Rationale: *Surgeons* is not a proper name so it does not need to be capitalized. A comma is not needed to break up a team of surgeons from the rest of the sentence. Option A is incorrect because a comma ,not a colon, is needed to set off an item. Option C is incorrect because *those* is an incorrect pronoun.

42. In addition to the feeling of accomplishment that the workers achieve, some jobs also give a sense of self- identity to the employees.
    (Easy) (Skill 6.2)

    A. achieve
    B. gave
    C. employees
    D. No change is necessary

    Answer: C -- employees

    Rationale: Option C is correct because *employees* is not possessive. Option A is incorrect because *achieve* is spelled correctly in the sentence. Option B is incorrect because *gave* is the wrong tense.

43. Profesions like law, education, and sales offer huge financial and emotional rewards.
    (Easy) (Skill 8.3)

    A. Professions
    B. education;
    C. offered
    D. No change is necessary

    Answer: A – Professions

    Rationale: Option A is correct because *professions* is misspelled in the sentence. Option B is incorrect because a comma, not a semi-colon, is needed after *education*. In Option C, *offered*, is in the wrong tense.

TEACHER CERTIFICATION STUDY GUIDE

44. Politicians <u>are</u> public <u>servants: who</u> <u>work</u> for the federal and state governments.
    (Average Rigor) (Skill 7.3)

    A. were
    B. servants who
    C. worked
    D. No change is necessary

    Answer: B – servants who

    Rationale: A colon is not needed to set off the introduction of the sentence. In Option A, *were*, is the incorrect tense of the verb. In Option C, *worked*, is in the wrong tense.

45. President <u>bush</u> is basically employed <u>by</u> the American people to <u>make</u> laws and run the country. *(Easy) (Skill 8.2)*

    A. Bush
    B. to
    C. made
    D. No change is necessary

    Answer: A – Bush

    Rationale: *Bush* is a proper name and should be capitalized. Option B, *to*, does not fit with the verb *employed*. Option C uses the wrong form of the verb, *make*.

46. <u>Finally;</u> the contributions that employees make to <u>their</u> companies and to the world cannot be <u>taken</u> for granted. *(Average Rigor) (Skill 7.3)*

    A. Finally,
    B. their
    C. took
    D. No change is necessary

    Answer: A – Finally,

    Rationale: A comma is needed to separate *Finally* from the rest of the sentence. Finally is a preposition which usually heads a dependent sentence, hence a comma is needed. Option B is incorrect because *their* is misspelled. Option C is incorrect because *took* is the wrong form of the verb.

DIRECTIONS: *For the underlined sentence(s), choose the option that expresses the meaning with the most fluency and the clearest logic within the context. If the underlined sentence should not be changed, choose Option A, which shows no change.*

47. **Selecting members of a President's cabinet can often be an aggravating process. <u>Either there are too many or too few qualified candidates for a certain position, and then they have to be confirmed by the Senate, where there is the possibility of rejection.</u>** *(Rigorous) (Skill 2.3 2.4, 14.1)*

    A. Either there are too many or too few qualified candidate for a certain position, and then they have to be confirmed by the Senate, where there is the possibility of rejection.
    B. Qualified candidates for certain positions face the possibility of rejection, when they have to be confirmed by the Senate.
    C. The Senate has to confirm qualified candidates, who face the possibility of rejection.
    D. Because the Senate has to confirm qualified candidates; they face the possibility of rejection.

    Answer: C -- The Senate has to confirm qualified candidates, who face the possibility of rejection

    Rationale: Option C is the most straightforward and concise sentence. Option A is too unwieldy with the wordy *Either...or* phrase at the beginning. Option B doesn't make clear the fact that candidates face rejection by the Senate. Option D illogically implies that candidates face rejection because they have to be confirmed by the Senate.

48. **Treating patients for drug and/or alcohol abuse is a sometimes difficult process. Even though there are a number of different methods for helping the patient overcome a dependency, there is no way of knowing which is best in the long-run.**
(Rigorous) (Skill 2.3, 2.4, 14.1)

   A. Even though there are a number of different methods for helping the patient overcome a dependency, there is no way of knowing which is best in the long-run.
   B. Even though different methods can help a patient overcome a dependency, there is no way to know which is best in the long-run.
   C. Even though there is no way to know which way is best in the long run, patients can overcome their dependencies when they are helped.
   D. There is no way to know which method will help the patient overcome a dependency in the long-run, even though there are many different ones.

   Answer: B -- Even though different methods can help a patient overcome a dependency, there is no way to know which is best in the long-run.

   Rationale: Option B is concise and logical. Option A tends to ramble with the use of *there are* and the verbs *helping* and *knowing*. Option C is awkwardly worded and repetitive in the first part of the sentence, and vague in the second because it never indicates how the patients can be helped. Option D contains the unnecessary phrase *even though there are many different ones*.

TEACHER CERTIFICATION STUDY GUIDE

49. Many factors account for the decline in quality of public education. <u>Overcrowding, budget cutbacks, and societal deterioration which have greatly affected student learning.</u>
    (Average Rigor) (Skill 2.3, 2.4, 14.1)

    A. Overcrowding, budget cutbacks, and societal deterioration which have greatly affected student learning.
    B. Student learning has been greatly affected by overcrowding, budget cutbacks, and societal deterioration.
    C. Due to overcrowding, budget cutbacks, and societal deterioration, student learning has been greatly affected.
    D. Overcrowding, budget cutbacks, and societal deterioration have affected students learning greatly.

    Answer: B -- Student learning has been greatly affected by overcrowding, budget cutbacks, and societal deterioration

    Rationale: Option B is concise and best explains the causes of the decline in student education. The unnecessary use of *which* in Option A makes the sentence feel incomplete. Option C has weak coordination between the reasons for the decline in public education and the fact that student learning has been affected. Option D incorrectly places the adverb *greatly* after learning, instead of before *affected*.

    DIRECTIONS: *Choose the sentence that logically and correctly expresses the comparison.*

50. *(Average Rigor) (Skill 6.3)*

    A. The Empire State Building in New York is taller than buildings in the city.
    B. The Empire State Building in New York is taller than any other building in the city.
    C. The Empire State Building in New York is tallest than other buildings in the city.

    Answer: B -- The Empire State Building in New York is taller than any other building in the city

    Rationale: Because the Empire State Building is a building in New York City, the phrase *any other* must be included. Option A is incorrect because the Empire State Building is implicitly compared to itself since it is one of the buildings. Option C is incorrect because *tallest* is the incorrect form of the adjective.

DIRECTIONS: *Choose the most ineffective word within the context of the sentence.*

51. **Considered by many to be** one of the worst **terrorist** incidents **on American soil** was the bombing of the Oklahoma City Federal Building which will be remembered **for years to come**. *(Average Rigor) (Skill 1.1)*

    A. considered by many to be
    B. terrorist
    C. on American soil
    D. for years to come

    Answer: A – considered by many to be

    Rationale: *Considered by many to be* is a wordy phrase and unnecessary in the context of the sentence. All other words are necessary within the context of the sentence.

52. The **flu** epidemic struck **most of** the **respected** faculty and students of The Woolbright School, forcing the Boynton Beach School Superintendent to close it down **for two weeks.** *(Average Rigor) (Skill 1.1)*

    A. flu
    B. most of
    C. respected
    D. for two weeks

    Answer: C -- respected

    Rationale: The fact that the faculty might have been *respected* is not really necessary to mention in the sentence. The other words and phrases are all necessary to complete the meaning of the sentence.

53. The <u>expanding</u> number of television channels has <u>prompted</u> cable operators to raise their prices, <u>even though</u> many consumers do not want to pay a higher <u>increased</u> amount for their service. *(Average Rigor) (Skill 1.1)*

   A. expanding
   B. prompted
   C. even though
   D. increased

   Answer: D -- increased

   Rationale: The word *increased* is redundant with higher and should be removed. All the other words are necessary within the context of the sentence.

   DIRECTIONS: Read the following paragraph and answer the questions that follow.

   This writer has often been asked to tutor hospitalized children with cystic fibrosis. While undergoing all the precautionary measures to see these children (i.e. scrubbing thoroughly and donning sterilized protective gear- for the child's protection), she has often wondered why their parents subject these children to the pressures of schooling and trying to catch up on what they have missed because of hospitalization, which is a normal part of cystic fibrosis patients' lives. These children undergo so many tortuous treatments a day that it seems cruel to expect them to learn as normal children do, especially with their life expectancies being as short as they are.

54. What is meant by the word "precautionary" in the second sentence? *(Average Rigor) (Skill 1.1)*

   A. Careful
   B. Protective
   C. Medical
   D. Sterilizing

   Answer: B – Protective

   Rationale: The writer uses expressions such as "protective gear" and "child's protection" to emphasize this.

55. **What is the main idea of this passage?** *(Rigorous) (Skill 2.4)*

   A. There is a lot of preparation involved in visiting a patient of cystic fibrosis.
   B. Children with cystic fibrosis are incapable of living normal lives.
   C. Certain concessions should be made for children with cystic fibrosis.
   D. Children with cystic fibrosis die young.

   Answer: C -- Certain concessions should be made for children with cystic fibrosis

   Rationale: The author states that she wonders "why parents subject these children to the pressures of schooling" and that "it seems cruel to expect them to learn as normal children do." In making these statements she appears to be expressing the belief that these children should not have to do what "normal" children do. They have enough to deal with – their illness itself.

56. **What is the author's tone?** *(Rigorous) (Skill 13.3)*

   A. Sympathetic
   B. Cruel
   C. Disbelieving
   D. Cheerful

   Answer: A -- Sympathetic

   Rationale: The author states that "it seems cruel to expect them to learn as normal children do," thereby indicating that she feels sorry for them.

57. **What is the author's purpose?** *(Rigorous) (Skill 13.3)*

   A. To inform
   B. To entertain
   C. To describe
   D. To narrate

   Answer: C – To describe

   Rationale: The author is simply describing her experience in working with children with cystic fibrosis.

58. **What type of organizational pattern is the author using?**
    (Rigorous) (Skill 3.1)

    A. Classification
    B. Explanation
    C. Comparison and contrast
    D. Cause and effect

    Answer: B -- Explanation

    Rationale: The author mentions tutoring children with cystic fibrosis in her opening sentence and goes on to "explain" some of these issues that are involved with her job.

59. **The author states that it is "cruel" to expect children with cystic fibrosis to learn as "normal" children do. Is this a fact or an opinion?**
    (Average Rigor) (Skill 4.3)

    A. Fact
    B. Opinion

    Answer: B -- Opinion

    Rationale: The fact that she states that it "seems" cruel indicates there is no evidence to support this belief.

60. **Is there evidence of bias in this paragraph?**
    (Average Rigor) (Skill 13.3)

    A. Yes
    B. No

    Answer: A -- Yes

    Rationale: The writer clearly feels sorry for these children and gears her writing in that direction.

61. **What kind of relationship is found within the last sentence which starts with "These children undergo..." and ends with "...as short as they are"?**
    (Rigorous) (Skill 3.1)

    A. Addition
    B. Explanation
    C. Generalization
    D. Classification

    Answer: B -- Explanation

    Rationale: In mentioning the their life expectancies are short, she is explaining by giving one reason why it is cruel to expect them to learn as normal children do.

62. **Does the author present an argument that is valid or invalid concerning the schooling of children with cystic fibrosis?** *(Rigorous) (Skill 13.3)*

    A. Valid
    B. Invalid

    Answer: B -- Invalid

    Rationale: Even though to most readers, the writer's argument makes good sense, it is biased and lacks real evidence.

    DIRECTIONS: Read the following passage and answer the questions that follow.

    Disciplinary practices have been found to affect diverse areas of child development such as the acquisition of moral values, obedience to authority, and performance at school. Even though the dictionary has a specific Definition of the word "discipline," it is still open to interpretation by people of different cultures.

    There are four types of disciplinary styles: assertion of power, withdrawal of love, reasoning, and permissiveness. Assertion of power involves the use of force to discourage unwanted behavior. Withdrawal of love involves making the love of a parent conditional on a child's good behavior. Reasoning involves persuading the child to behave one way rather than another. Permissiveness involves allowing the child to do as he or she pleases and face the consequences of his/her actions.

TEACHER CERTIFICATION STUDY GUIDE

63. **What is the meaning of the word "diverse" in the first sentence?**
    (Easy) (Skill 1.1)
    A. Many
    B. Related to children
    C. Disciplinary
    D. Moral

    Answer: A -- Many

    Rationale: Any of the other choices would be redundant in this sentence.

64. **Name the four types of disciplinary styles.**
    (Easy) (Skill 2.0)

    A. Reasoning, power assertion, morality, and permissiveness.
    B. Morality, reasoning, permissiveness, and withdrawal of love.
    C. Withdrawal of love, permissiveness, assertion of power, and reasoning.
    D. Permissiveness, morality, reasoning, and power assertion.

    Answer: C -- Withdrawal of love, permissiveness, assertion of power, and reasoning.

    Rationale: This is directly stated in the second paragraph.

65. **What organizational structure is used in the first sentence of the second paragraph?**
    (Average Rigor) (Skill 13.3)

    A. Addition
    B. Explanation
    C. Definition
    D. Simple listing

    Answer: D – Simple listing

    Rationale: The author simply states the types of disciplinary styles.

TEACHER CERTIFICATION STUDY GUIDE

66. **What is the main idea of this passage?**
    (Rigorous) (Skill 2.1)

    A. Different people have different ideas of what discipline is.
    B. Permissiveness is the most widely used disciplinary style.
    C. Most people agree on their definition of discipline.
    D. There are four disciplinary styles.

    Answer: A – Different people have different ideas of what discipline is

    Rationale: Choice C is not true, the opposite is stated in the passage. Choice B could be true, but we have no evidence of this. Choice D is just one of the many facts listed in the passage.

67. **Is this passage biased?**
    (Rigorous) (Skill 13.3)

    A. Yes
    B. No

    Answer: B – No

    Rationale: If the reader were so inclined, he could research discipline and find this information.

68. **What is the author's tone?** *(Rigorous) (Skill 13.3)*

    A. Disbelieving
    B. Angry
    C. Informative
    D. Optimistic

    Answer: C -- Informative

    Rationale: The author appears to simply be stating the facts.

69. **The author states that "assertion of power involves the use of force to discourage unwanted behavior." Is this a fact or an opinion?**
    (Average Rigor) (Skill 4.3)

    A. Fact
    B. Opinion

    Answer: A -- Fact

    Rationale: The author appears to have done extensive research on this subject.

70. **From reading this passage we can conclude that**
    (Average Rigor) (Skill 13.3)

    A. The author is a teacher.
    B. The author has many children.
    C. The author has written a book about discipline.
    D. The author has done a lot of research on discipline.

    Answer: D – The author has done a lot of research on discipline

    Rationale: Given all the facts mentioned in the passage, this is the only inference one can make.

    DIRECTIONS: Read the following passage and answer the questions that follow.

    One of the most difficult problems plaguing American education is the assessment of teachers. No one denies that teachers ought to be answerable for what they do, but what exactly does that mean? The Oxford American Dictionary defines accountability as: the obligation to give a reckoning or explanation for one's actions.

    Does a student have to learn for teaching to have taken place? Historically, teaching has not been defined in this restrictive manner; the teacher was thought to be responsible for the quantity and quality of material covered and the way in which it was presented. However, some definitions of teaching now imply that students must learn in order for teaching to have taken place.

    As a teacher who tries my best to keep current on all the latest teaching strategies, I believe that those teachers who do not bother even to pick up an educational journal every once in a while should be kept under close watch. There are many teachers out there who have been teaching for decades and refuse to change their ways even if research has proven that their methods are outdated and ineffective. There is no place in the profession of teaching for these types of individuals. It is time that the American educational system clean house, for the sake of our children.

71. **What is the meaning of the word "reckoning" in the third sentence?**
    (Easy) (Skill 1.1)

    A. Thought
    B. Answer
    C. Obligation
    D. Explanation

    Answer: D -- Explanation

    Rationale: The meaning of this word is directly stated in the same sentence.

72. **What is the main idea of the passage?**
    (Rigorous) (Skill 2.1)

    A. Teachers should not be answerable for what they do.
    B. Teachers who do not do their job should be fired.
    C. The author is a good teacher.
    D. Assessment of teachers is a serious problem in society today.

    Answer: D – Assessment of teachers is a serious problem in society today.

    Rationale: Most of the passage is dedicated to elaborating on why teacher assessment is such a problem.

73. **From the passage, one can infer that**
    (Rigorous) (Skill 13.3)

    A. The author considers herself a good teacher.
    B. Poor teachers will be fired.
    C. Students have to learn for teaching to take place.
    D. The author will be fired.

    Answer: A – The author considers herself a good teacher.

    Rationale: The first sentence of the third paragraph alludes to this.

74. **Teachers who do not keep current on educational trends should be fired. Is this a fact or an opinion?**
    (Average Rigor) (Skill 4.3)

    A. Fact
    B. Opinion

    Answer: B -- Opinion

    Rationale: There may be those who feel they can be good teachers by using old methods.

TEACHER CERTIFICATION STUDY GUIDE

75. The author states that teacher assessment is a problem for
    (Average Rigor) (Skill 13.3)

    A. Elementary schools
    B. Secondary schools
    C. American education
    D. Families

    Answer: C – American education

    Rationale: This fact is directly stated in the first paragraph.

76. What is the author's purpose in writing this?
    (Average Rigor) (Skill 13.3)

    A. To entertain
    B. To narrate
    C. To describe
    D. To persuade

    Answer: D – To persuade

    Rationale: The author does some describing, but the majority of her statements seemed geared towards convincing the reader that teachers who are lazy or who do not keep current should be fired.

77. Is there evidence of bias in this passage?
    (Rigorous) (Skill 13.3)

    A. Yes
    B. No

    Answer: A -- Yes

    Rationale: The entire third paragraph is the author's opinion on the matter.

78. What is the author's overall organizational pattern?
    (Rigorous) (Skill 13.3)

    A. Classification
    B. Cause and effect
    C. Definition
    D. Comparison and contrast

    Answer: C -- Definition

    Rationale: The author identifies teacher assessment as a problem and spends the rest of the passage defining why it is considered a problem.

79. The author's tone is one of
    (Rigorous) (Skill 13.3)

    A. Disbelief
    B. Excitement
    C. Support
    D. Concern

    Answer: D -- Concern

    Rationale: The author appears concerned with the future of education.

80. What is meant by the word "plaguing" in the first sentence?
    (Average Rigor) (Skill 1.1)

    A. Causing problems
    B. Causing illness
    C. Causing anger
    D. Causing failure

    Answer: A – Causing problems

    Rationale: The first paragraph makes this definition clear.

TEACHER CERTIFICATION STUDY GUIDE

81. **Where does the author get her definition of "accountability?"**
    (Average Rigor) (Skill 1.1)

    A. Webster's Dictionary
    B. Encyclopedia Britannica
    C. Oxford Dictionary
    D. World Book Encyclopedia

    Answer: C – Oxford Dictionary

    Rationale: This is directly stated in the third sentence of the first paragraph.

82. **What development patterns should a professional teacher assess to meet the needs of the students?**
    (Rigorous) (Skill 13.1)

    A. Academic, regional and family background
    B. Social, physical, academic
    C. Academic, physical and family background
    D. Physical, family and ethnic background

    Answer: B – Social, physical, academic

    Rationale: The effective teacher applies knowledge of physical, social, and academic developmental patterns and of individual differences, to meet the instructional needs of all students in the classroom and. The most important premise of child development is that all domains of development (physical, social, and academic) are integrated. The teacher has a broad knowledge and thorough understanding of the development that typically occurs during the students' current period of life. More importantly, the teacher understands how children learn best during each period of development. An examination of the student's file coupled with ongoing evaluation assures a successful educational experience for both teacher and students.

TEACHER CERTIFICATION STUDY GUIDE

83. **The use of technology in the classroom allows for**
    (Average Rigor) (Skill 13.2)

    A.   More complex lessons
    B.   Better delivery of instruction
    C.   Variety of instruction
    D.   Better ability to meet more individual student needs

    Answer: D – Better ability to meet more individual student needs

    Rationale: Using technology, the teacher can incorporate more than one learning style into a lesson. In this way, the teacher can meet the individual needs of the students more effectively.

84. **To promote word study, children can**
    (Average Rigor) (Skill 13.2)

    A.   Be required to go to the dictionary at least once or twice a day.
    B.   Collect and share words of interest they find in their readings.
    C.   Do vocabulary work sheets from a basal reader or commercial vocabulary book.
    D.   Do all of the above.

    Answer: D – Do all of the above

    Rationale: All of the answers promote student word study.

85. **How can students use a computer desktop publishing center?**
    (Average Rigor) (Skill 13.2)

    A.   To set up a classroom budget
    B.   To create student made books
    C.   To design a research project
    D.   To create a classroom behavior management system

    Answer: B – To create student made books

    Rationale: To create student made books. By creating a book, students gain new insights into how communication works. Suddenly, the concept of audience for what they write and create becomes real. They also have an opportunity to be introduced to graphic arts, an exploding field. In addition, just as computers are a vital part of the world they will be entering as adults, so is desktop publishing. It is universally used by businesses of all kinds.

86. **To help students with "main idea" questions, the teacher should**
    (Average Rigor) (Skill 13.3)

    A. Give out a strategy sheet on the main idea for children to place their Rader's notebooks.
    B. Model responding to such a question as part of guided reading.
    C. Have children create "main idea questions" to go with their writings
    D. All of the above.

    Answer: D – All of the above

    Rationale: All of these strategies help students identify the main ideas in reading passages.

87. **Dictionary study**
    (Average Rigor) (Skill 13.2)

    A. Can begin in grades 1 or 2.
    B. Can begin in pre-K using the lush picture dictionaries.
    C. Should start on grade three level.
    D. A and b.

    Answer: D – A and B

    Rationale: Dictionary study can begin in pre-k because of the picture dictionaries.

88. **Children "own" words when all of the following happen except**
    (Average Rigor) (Skill 13.2)

    A. They find these words on their own.
    B. The teacher provides a mandated word list.
    C. They use the words in their own writings.
    D. The words appear in literature that interests them.

    Answer: B -- The teacher provides a mandated word list

    Rationale: Memorizing a list of words out of context is not effective teaching.

89. One of the many ways in which a child can demonstrate comprehension of a story is by:
    (Average rigor) *(Skill 13.3)*

    A. Filling in a strategy sheet.
    B. Retelling the story orally.
    C. Retelling the story in writing.
    D. All of the above.

    Answer: D -- All of the above

    Rationale: All the options are good ones.

90. Making inferences from the text means that the reader:
    (Rigorous) *(Skill 13.3)*

    A. Is making informed judgments based on available evidence.
    B. Is making a guess based on prior experiences.
    C. Is making a guess based on what the reader would like to be true of the text.
    D. All of the above

    Answer: A -- Is making informed judgments based on available evidence.

    Rationale: This is a definition question that a literate test taker can answer based on the general definition of inferences

TEACHER CERTIFICATION STUDY GUIDE

STATE MAJOR COMPONENTS RETAINED AND CHANGES OF IDEA 2004

The second revision of IDEA occurred in 2004, when IDEA was re-authorized as the Individuals with Disabilities Education Improvement Act of 2004 (IDEIA 2004). It is commonly referred to as IDEA 2004. IDEA 2004 was effective July 1, 2005.

It was the intention to improve IDEA by adding the philosophy and understanding that special education students need preparation for further study beyond the high school setting by teaching compensatory methods. Accordingly, IDEA 2004 provided a close tie to PL 89-10, the Elementary and Special Education Act of 1965, and stated that students with special needs should have maximum access to the general curriculum. This was defined as the amount for an individual student to reach his fullest potential. Full inclusion was stated not to be the only option by which to achieve this, and specified that skills should be taught to compensate students later in life in cases where inclusion was not the best setting.

IDEA 2004 added a new requirement for special education teachers on the secondary level enforcing NCLB's "Highly Qualified" requirements in the subject area of their curriculum. The rewording in this part of IDEA states that they shall be "no less qualified" than teachers in the core areas.

Free and Appropriate Public Education (FAPE) was revised by mandating that students have maximum access to appropriate general education. Additionally, LRE placement for those students with disabilities must have the same school placement rights as those students who are not disabled. IDEA 2004 recognizes that due to the nature of some disabilities, appropriate education may vary in the amount of participation/placement in the general education setting. For some students, FAPE will mean a choice as to the type of educational institution they attend (private school for example), any of which must provide the special education services deemed necessary for the student through the IEP.

The definition of *assistive technology devices* was amended to exclude devices that are surgically implanted (i.e. cochlear implants), and clarified that students with assistive technology devices shall not be prevented from having special education services. Assistive technology devices may need to monitored by school personnel, but schools are not responsible for the implantation or replacement of such devices surgically. An example of this would be a cochlear implant.

The definition of *child with a disability* is the term used for children ages 3-9 with a developmental delay now has been was changed to allow for the inclusion of Tourettes Syndrome.

ASSESS. OF TEACH. ASSIST. SKILLS

IDEA 2004 recognized that all states must follow the National Instructional Materials Accessibility Standards which states that students who need materials in a certain form will get those at the same time their non-disabled peers receive their materials. Teacher recognition of this standard is important.

Changes in Requirements for Evaluations

The clock/time allowance between the request for an initial evaluation and the determination if a disability is present may be requested has been changed to state the finding/determination must occur within 60 calendar days of the request. This is a significant change as previously it was interpreted to mean 60 school days. Parental consent is also required for evaluations and prior to the start of special education services.

No single assessment or measurement tool may now be used to determine special education qualification. Assessments and measurements used should be in *language and form* that will give the most accurate picture of the child's abilities.

IDEA 2004 recognized that there exists a disproportionate representation of minorities and bilingual students and that pre-service interventions that are *scientifically based on early reading programs, positive behavioral interventions and support, and early intervening services* may prevent some of those children from needing special education services. This understanding has led to a child not being considered to have a disability if he/she has not had appropriate education in math or reading, nor shall a child be considered to have a disability if the reason for his/her delays is that English is a second language.

When determining a specific learning disability, the criteria may or may not use a discrepancy between *achievement and intellectual ability* but whether or not the child responds to scientific research-based intervention. In general, children who may not have been found eligible for special education (via testing) but are known to need services (via functioning, excluding lack of instruction) are still eligible for special education services. This change now allows input for evaluation to include state and local testing, classroom observation, academic achievement, and *related developmental need.*,

Changes in Requirements for IEPs

Individualized Education Plans (IEPS) continue to have multiple sections. One section, *present levels,* now addresses *academic achievement and functional performance.* Annual IEP goals must now address the same areas.

IEP goals should be aligned to state standards; thus short term objectives are not required on every IEP. Students with IEPs must not only participate in regular education programs to the full extent possible, they must show progress in those programs. This means that goals should be written to reflect academic progress.

For students who must participate in alternate assessment, there must be alignment to *alternate achievement standards.*

Significant change has been made in the definition of the IEP team as it now includes *not less than 1* teacher from each of the areas of special education and regular education be present.

IDEA 2004 recognized that the amount of required paperwork placed upon teachers of students with disabilities should be reduced if possible; for this reason a pilot program has been developed in which some states will participate using multi-year IEPs. Individual student inclusion in this program will require consent by both the school and the parent.

XAMonline, INC. 21 Orient Ave. Melrose, MA 02176
Toll Free number 800-509-4128
TO ORDER Fax 781-662-9268 OR www.XAMonline.com
<u>NEW YORK STATE TEACHER CERTIFICATION</u>
<u>EXAMINATION - NYSTCE - 2008</u>
PO#   Store/School:

Address 1:

Address 2 (Ship to other):
City, State Zip

Credit card number_____-_____-_____-_____   expiration_____
EMAIL _____
PHONE   **FAX**

ISBN	TITLE	Qty	Retail	Total
978-1-58197-866-7	NYSTCE ATS-W ASSESSMENT OF TEACHING SKILLS- WRITTEN 91			
978-1-58197-260-3	NYSTCE ATAS ASSESSMENT OF TEACHING ASSISTANT SKILLS 095			
978-1-58197-289-4	CST BIOLOGY 006			
978-1-58197-855-1	CST CHEMISTRY 007			
978-1-58197-865-0	CQST COMMUNICATION AND QUANTITATIVE SKILLS TEST 080			
978-1-58197-632-8	CST EARTH SCIENCE 008			
978-1-58197-267-2	CST ENGLISH 003			
978-1-58197-858-2	CST FRENCH SAMPLE TEST 012			
978-1-58197-344-0	LAST LIBERAL ARTS AND SCIENCE TEST 001			
978-1-58197-863-6	CST LIBRARY MEDIA SPECIALIST 074			
978-1-58197-623-6	CST LITERACY 065			
978-1-58197-296-2	CST MATH 004			
978-1-58197-290-0	CST MUTIPLE SUBJECTS 002			
978-1-58197-864-3	CST PHYSICAL EDUCATION 076			
978-1-58197-873-5	CST PHYSICS 009			
978-1-58197-265-8	CST SOCIAL STUDIES 005			
978-1-58197-619-9	CST SPANISH 020			
978-1-58197-258-0	CST STUDENTS WITH DISABILITIES 060			
			SUBTOTAL	
	FOR PRODUCT PRICES VISIT WWW.XAMONLINE.COM		Ship	$8.25
			TOTAL	

www.ingramcontent.com/pod-product-compliance
Lightning Source LLC
Chambersburg PA
CBHW080540300426
44111CB00017B/2810